The SEARCH —for— MEANING

Thomas H. Naylor
William H. Willimon
Magdalena R. Naylor

Abingdon Press
Nashville

THE SEARCH FOR MEANING

This book is printed on acid-free, recycled paper.

Library of Congress Cataloging-in-Publication Data

Naylor, Thomas H., 1936–
    The search for meaning/Thomas H. Naylor, William H. Willimon, Magdalena R. Naylor.
        p.   cm.
ISBN 0-687-08176-9 (alk. paper)
    1. Life. 2. Meaning (Philosophy) 3. Spiritual life.
I. Willimon, William H. II. Naylor, Magdalena R., 1950—
III. Title.
BD435.N39   1994
128—dc20
                                                                    93-23618
                                                                    CIP

00 01 02 03—10 9 8 7 6 5 4

MANUFACTURED IN THE UNITED STATES OF AMERICA

Contents

Preface

Ten minutes after the bombing began in Baghdad on the evening of January 16, 1991, students began trickling into a Duke University classroom to participate in a new seminar, "The Search for Meaning." Operation Desert Storm had begun and so had a 14-week journey involving an economist, a theologian, and fifteen undergraduate students. Against the somber background of the Persian Gulf War and its aftershocks, we pondered the meaning of an uncertain future. Why are we here? Where are we going? What does it all mean? These were among the questions with which we struggled. Not knowing where we were going or where we might end up, the seminar proved to be the most challenging teaching experience of our respective careers.

Shaken by the news of the Gulf War, the students were quite open and vocal during the first evening—a pattern that persisted throughout the semester. The group included three Roman Catholics, a Jew, several Southern Baptists, a Chinese agnostic, three or four "nonbelievers," and a young man who grew up in Beirut reared by Jesuits. They all felt they had the right to challenge every word that we said—and they did.

Noting that sometimes, in a university, students become knowledgeable in every possible subject except life and how to live it, we proposed to read several books together, study some speeches and a play, and have lots of discussion on the theme, "How do people find meaning in life?" Unhappy with the limitations of the restricted, departmentalized university curriculum, we sought a course which would be integrative, personal, engaging, and demanding. After the first semester we were joined in our search by a psychiatrist. This book is the result of what the three of us have learned from leading "The Search for Meaning" seminar at Duke and elsewhere.

For two of us, Will and Thomas, our quest evolved out of our personal experiences in the South in the 1950s with state-imposed racial segregation and Protestantism. Will's spiritual trek has been that of a United Methodist pastor, professor, and university chaplain.

---

*M*y search for meaning has involved a lifelong commitment to the church through various forms of ministry. While I resonate to the challenge, voiced repeatedly throughout this book, to take personal, active responsibility for one's search for meaning, for me this search has meant engagement with the scriptures, traditions, and congregational embodiment of the Christian faith. The challenge for me in this book has been to relate my specific Christian convictions to a dialogue with and assistance in the search for meaning from those who do not share all of my convictions.   THE PASTOR

As a tolerant agnostic who rarely attended religious services, Thomas's pursuit of life's meaning lay dormant for almost twenty-five years after he left Mississippi. However, his search received an infusion of new energy from a spiritual encounter with a young Communist woman—a professed atheist—outside the Kremlin walls in Moscow in 1982.

Magdalena grew up in an environment that was far more repressive than that experienced by Thomas and Will. Her quest began in Warsaw, Poland, where for thirty years she lived under the combination of Stalinist communism and Polish Catholicism. After completing medical school and a Ph.D. in cardiovascular physiology, she began having second thoughts about the dehumanizing aspects of high tech medicine and medical research in Poland and in the United States. Her search for a more humanistic form of medicine led her to psychiatry.

Shortly after this book was written, Magdalena and Thomas compared the quality of their life in Richmond, Virginia, with the type of life-style about which they had written. They concluded that they either had to rewrite the book or their life-style had to be changed. They now live in Vermont.

*A*fter returning from my 1982 trip to Moscow, I approached a local minister with the proposition, "May I join your church, if I accept most of the theology of the New Testament, but have problems with some of the stories?" "Welcome to the search," he responded. As a searching Episcopalian, I find myself attracted to Jesus Christ's message of love and community. However, I still have a lot of questions about God. Is there a God? Who is this God? Is God loving, caring, narcissistic, tyrannical, or vengeful? What is the meaning of God? The mysteries surrounding these questions and others draw me to the search.   THE ECONOMIST

Americans are "always on the way to someplace else," says *Harper's* editor Lewis H. Lapham.

If America is about nothing else, it is about the invention of the self. Because we have little use for history, and because we refuse the comforts of a society established on the blueprint of class privilege, we find ourselves set adrift at birth in an existential void, inheriting nothing except the obligation to construct a plausible self, to build a raft of identity. . . . Who else is the American hero if not a wandering pilgrim who goes forth on a perpetual quest?[1]

The search for meaning is in our bones, says Lapham. We therefore invite you to continue, to resume, maybe even to begin the most important pilgrimage of your life. In the following pages we will analyze why we think meaning is a problem, perhaps the central problem of modern people. Then we will lead you through a step-by-step process of looking for meaning in your life and in setting some specific goals and objectives for your search. Whether read alone or with a group of friends, we believe this book can enrich your life, not by any secret wisdom we have to offer, but rather by its encouragement to see yourself again as a pilgrim on the way to someplace else.

*W*ith my strong Roman Catholic background, I have little difficulty believing in a higher power. However, the nature of this power is a mystery to me. I have trouble rationalizing the tremendous amount of pain and suffering in the world in light of the optimistic message of the New Testament. Although I am an Episcopalian, for me the search for meaning is *not* synonymous with the search for God. My search has been honed by my personal psychoanalysis, and it continues through the psychotherapy with my patients.

THE PSYCHIATRIST

This book is an invitation to you to join our journey. We encourage you to take hold of your life, to take an honest look at where you are going and where you hope to go. Together, we shall look over the shoulders of others who are engaged in the search. We shall be pilgrims on the way to a new place of being.

To our students at Duke University and elsewhere, we dedicate this book. If they had not been willing to journey with us, we would never have set out in the first place.

In addition to our students and workshop participants, several others made significant contributions to this book. Virtually every idea contained in the book benefited from weekly discussions with Jack D. DeLoyht, who also contributed two poems. Denise Skellett typed endless revisions of the manuscript. Comments and encouragement from the Reverend James R. Adams, Dr. Diana Antonacci, Edward B. Briggs, Dr. Daniel Gianturco, Dr. Marvin L. Hage, Norman Lear, Dr. Richard Lucas, Dr. Friedrich Rosenkranz, the Reverend William L. Sachs, Keith Sinzinger, Rabbi Jack D. Spiro, and Kip Thompson were particularly helpful. The invaluable assistance of our agent, Donald C. Brandenburgh, is gratefully acknowledged.

Thomas H. Naylor
William H. Willimon
Magdalena R. Naylor

THE LIVING DEAD

The search is what anyone would undertake if he were not sunk in the everydayness of his own life. . . . To become aware of the possibility of the search is to be onto something. Not to be onto something is to be in despair.

WALKER PERCY
THE MOVIEGOER

We are living in the midst of a spiritual crisis of unprecedented proportions.[1] The demise of communism and the collapse of the Soviet Union have unmistakably exposed our psychological vulnerability. We have no idea what we want to be now that the cold war is over. Our nation has lost its way. We suffer from meaninglessness, which in turn leads to separation, alienation, and ultimately to despair. The same is true for much of Europe—particularly France, Germany, Italy, Sweden, and most of Eastern Europe—not to mention all of the former Soviet republics. Our political, spiritual, academic, and business leaders have no vision of the future. We have no sense of community. The specter of nihilism looms over us.

Those who are alienated attempt to defend themselves by being detached from their families, their work, their government, their basic beliefs, and eventually themselves. Drug abuse, alcoholism, divorce, sexual abuse, teenage suicide, crime, and violence are all rooted in meaninglessness. Why are the lives of so many people living in Western industrial nations void of meaning? What, if anything, can be done about this egregious problem? We can't begin to deal with meaninglessness, if we don't recognize it even when it's staring us in the face.

Nowhere is meaninglessness more prevalent than on college campuses. Colleges and universities have lost their bearing—administrators, faculty, and students. "Duke University is a world-class university—far superior to Princeton," proclaimed a Duke senior to a startled fundraising group. "It is one of the few major universities where it is possible to get drunk four nights a week for four years and still maintain a B average." To support his claim he cited the recent visit of four of his Princeton buddies, who confirmed that Duke is indeed a premier party school. Was this what the author of a cover page article in the *New York Times Magazine* had in mind when he described Duke as a "hot college"?

However, an article in the *Princeton Alumni Weekly* entitled "Drinking: A Sobering Look at an Enduring Princeton Pastime," casts doubt on Duke's alleged competitive advantage. The social scene at Duke or Princeton differs little from that of other American universities. A U.S. Surgeon General study found that our nation's college students drink nearly four billion cans of beer and enough wine and liquor to bring their annual consumption of alcoholic beverages up to thirty-four gallons a person. The widely publicized University of Virginia fraternity-house drug raids followed by reports of female striptease artists performing oral sex to entertain freshman rushees represent more of the same. College students suffer from a more fundamental malaise than alcohol and drug abuse. Their lives are meaningless.

For several years, M.B.A. students in Duke's Fuqua School of Business were asked to write a personal strategic plan. The question posed to them was, "What do you want to be when you grow up?" With few exceptions, they wanted three things—money, power, and things—very big things, including vacation homes, expensive foreign automobiles, yachts, and even airplanes. Primarily concerned with their careers and the growth of their financial portfolios, their personal plans contained little room for family, intellectual development, spiritual growth, or social responsibility.

Their mandate to the faculty was, "Teach me how to be a moneymaking machine." Technology—particularly the personal computer (PC)—was their god. Mesmerized by the silent hum of a smoothly running PC, they held to the illusion that they could deny their mortality and control their destiny.

These are the circumstances of the search for meaning in today's world. The search involves coming to grips with what it is to be a human being who lives, loves, works, plays, suffers, and dies. A strong sense of meaning is what motivates us to get out of bed each morning and confront yet another day of life and all its uncertainty, to transform our fate into our destiny, to make life more an adventure than a bore.

Few writers were more obsessed with the search for meaning than Albert Camus, who said, "The meaning of life is the most urgent of questions."[2] The appeal of the search is the lure of life's mystery itself. In the words of Reinhold Niebuhr, "The mystery of life is comprehended in meaning, though no human statement of the meaning can fully resolve the mystery."[3] Or, "To know that there is meaning but not to know the meaning, that is bliss,"[4] according to J. Middleton Murry.

Most colleges—in response to market pressures—are so preoccupied with careerism that they do little to facilitate students' search for meaning. The absence of meaning leads to drunken fraternity-house bashes, date rape, vandalism, and acts of violence. The indictment of a Duke student for date rape and a barroom knifing brawl were the lead stories of a recent Valentine's Day issue of the daily student newspaper—the *Duke Chronicle*.

Students have no incentive to delay gratification, because they place so little faith in the future that has no meaning for them. Instead, they pursue the elusive dream that it is possible "to have it all and to have it now"—a dream that turns out to be a lie, a materialistic cover for a lack of meaning.

While subscribing to an ideology that raises individualism to almost godlike status, most college students behave as world-class conformists. Some have tried—often in vain—to find meaning through the approval of parents, excessive television viewing, rock music, spectator sports, physical fitness, sexual promiscuity, and racism. Ironically, lacking any sense of direction, any inner conviction about what their lives ought to mean, they become the compliant victims of external pressures. Their parents, their passions, and the corporation pull their strings.

The college campus mirrors the conclusions of a study made by the American Medical Association and the National Association of State Boards of Education. "Never before has one generation of American teen-agers been less healthy, less cared-for or less prepared for life than their parents were at the same age." More than half of the students attending junior or senior high schools drink alcoholic beverages and almost half a million go on a drinking spree every week. Many are already alcoholics. The situation is even worse in Eastern Europe and in many former Soviet republics.

The rate of violent crimes by youth in the United States rose by 25 percent during the 1980s. The teenage suicide rate has tripled over the past three decades. Suicide is the second leading cause of death among fifteen-to-nineteen-year-olds. A Gallup Poll found that 15 percent of American teenagers have seriously considered suicide and that 6 percent have actually tried it. More than 70 percent of teenage suicides involve the frequent use of alcohol or drugs.

Campus life is a metaphor for our malaise. Prosperity and the availability of too much leisure time have given us more freedom than we know what to do with. As Erich Fromm once said, "We are a society of notoriously unhappy people: lonely, anxious, depressed, destructive, dependent—people who are glad when we have killed the time we are trying so hard to save."[5]

Although many mental illnesses can be traced to meaninglessness, countless people experience vacuous lives without any of the usual symptoms. Even though we live in a period of unprecedented prosperity, novelist Walker Percy warns that it is the Time of Thanatos—a time of the *living dead* in which "people who seem to be living lives which are good by all sociological standards . . . somehow seem to be more dead than alive."[6] As Percy said, "There is something worse than being deprived of life: it is being deprived of life and not knowing it."[7]

Many who are physically alive appear to be spiritually, emotionally, and intellectually dead. The living dead can be found everywhere—glued to CNN hour after hour hoping for an event in an uneventful life, reciting religious creeds in which they do not believe on Sunday morning, playing golf at the country club, working on an assembly line, saying "Have a nice day," spending endless hours in shopping malls, commuting to work, feigning interest in mindless bureaucratic jobs, being mesmerized by rock music, sunning themselves at the beach, sitting through uninspiring classroom lectures, and watching the Washington Redskins on TV in the neighborhood sports bar. It's not by chance alone that the average American spends twenty-eight hours a week watching TV or that cable television viewers will soon be able to choose from among 500 channels.

> *For* most people, life is the search for the correct manila folder to get filed away in.
>
> CLIFTON FADIMAN

There may be no escape from spiritual emptiness, unless one learns to ask the right questions:

Why am I here?
Where am I going?
What is the purpose of life?
Is there a God?
What will happen when I die?
Is there life after death?

These questions have in common a longing for a sense of grounding, purpose, or meaning in life. As human beings we have an insatiable need for assurance that the spiritual, intellectual, emotional, and physiological dimensions of our lives are connected to something meaningful. Our dilemma is that we live in a world in which life's meaning has not been self-evidently revealed to us. No matter how intense our desire for meaning, meaning eludes us.

In Kurt Vonnegut's *Cat's Cradle*, God has just created Adam. "What is the purpose of all this?" man asked politely. "Everything must have a purpose?" answered God. "Certainly," said man. "Then I'll leave it to you to think of one for all this," said God. And he went away. Or as Elie Wiesel has noted, when Adam first opened his eyes he asked God, "Who am I?" rather than "Who are you?"[8]

Some people seldom think about life's weighty questions. Others either deny their importance or accept dogmatic answers offered by "common sense" or various religious faiths. The psychological denial of life's important questions can lead to a plethora of existential anxieties, which may trigger various forms of debilitating mental illness. Although religious dogmas may provide temporary solace from the anxiety associated with the uncertainty of life's meaning, relief of this sort is often cut short by some personal crisis such as the death of a loved one, a severe financial setback, or a natural disaster. The inability to rationalize uncontrollable events through one's religious beliefs can shatter one's faith leaving one vulnerable to depression and other types of psychopathy. But there is another option, which is neither denial nor blind acceptance of conventional wisdom. It involves confronting life's ultimate questions head on and continuously searching for answers. The quest.

Too little attention is devoted to the open discussion of life's fundamental questions in our homes, religious institutions, schools, and universities. It is almost as if there were a vast conspiracy to talk about everything but matters of importance. People are afraid to express their doubts about conventional wisdom. Parents, teachers, and the clergy are reluctant to admit their inability to provide answers to questions about meaning. But that is precisely why we need to spend more time expressing our very real concerns about such issues. It is just as important to know what we don't know about meaning as it is to know what we do.

The quest for meaning gets to the essence of what life is all about—*the care and nurturing of our soul.* We will never find meaning if we pretend there is no problem and that the questions will just fade away. The search is no bed of roses. It may be painful, stressful, and very difficult. Although we do not promise "meaning kits" for those who stay the course, many find the journey to be a source of great joy and boundless energy. Life itself compels us to join the quest.

Welcome to the search!

Chapter 1

A SEARCH PROCESS

How does a being who needs meaning find meaning in a universe that has no meaning?

IRVIN D. YALOM
EXISTENTIAL PSYCHOTHERAPY

The Fable of the Deserted Island

*I*magine you are a European on a voyage of discovery during the time before Columbus. Your ship is destroyed by a violent storm. You are the lone survivor. Miraculously, the piece of the ship's debris to which you have been clinging since the ship went down washes ashore onto an uninhabited tropical island.

The lush island is full of fruits, nuts, and berries, an abundance of wildlife, and plenty of fresh water. There are caves to protect you from storms and animals. Physical survival poses no problem.

There is only one hitch. Not only are you the island's only inhabitant, but no one knows that you are there. You are presumed to have been lost at sea. There is no reason whatsoever to assume that another ship will ever pass your way before you die, since Europeans have not yet discovered America and such voyages are rare. You will never see another human being for the rest of your life.

From this grim tale several troubling questions emerge. How would you survive emotionally on such an island? What would you do? Could you find meaning there? If so, what form would it take? How would you choose to live your life? What if anything would make your life worthwhile? Is it possible to have a meaningful life without any human interaction whatsoever? What would prevent you from going mad? Would suicide be ruled out?

The questions about life's meaning for which the island demands answers are no different from the questions raised by life on our own island—the planet Earth. The island is a metaphor for life itself. Life on the island may be no worse than that of what Walker Percy calls the living dead. The quest for meaning, whether on the island or elsewhere, is a search for grounding and connectedness linking the spiritual, intellectual, emotional, and physiological dimensions of one's life.

The Life Matrix

For those who are trying to come to terms with the meaning of their life, we offer a search process. This process is aimed at college students, young professionals, homemakers, business executives, educators, the clergy, those involved in a mid-life crisis, those who don't know what to do with their life, and senior citizens reflecting on what to do in retirement. The search for meaning is for anyone with enough courage to search.

One of the reasons why many people find the search to be so elusive is that they don't understand the choices available to them. To help sort out these options and evaluate their spiritual, intellectual, emotional, and physiological consequences, we employ a simple matrix, which we call the *life matrix*. It identifies four different states of meaning—meaninglessness, separation, having, and being. These states are intended to be not rigid, mutually exclusive categories, but rather useful images to help us differentiate among the alternatives from which we may choose. The elements of the matrix represent the likely effects associated with a particular state of meaning. For example, it is not uncommon for someone for whom life has no meaning to experience depression, despair, and eventually death.

On a given day one may encounter all four of these states of meaning—moving from one state to another in response to mood shifts or changes in the external environment. The order in which the states appear in the life matrix does not reflect a particular hierarchy of importance. However, some have suggested that sepa-

THE LIFE MATRIX

STATES OF MEANING / EFFECTS	MEANINGLESSNESS	SEPARATION	HAVING	BEING
SPIRITUAL	DESPAIR	DETACHMENT	ORTHODOXY	QUEST
INTELLECTUAL	NIHILISM	ALIENATION	HEDONISM	GROWTH
EMOTIONAL	DEPRESSION	ANXIETY	NARCISSISM	BALANCE
PHYSIOLOGICAL	DEATH	SOMATIZATION	HEALTH FETISHISM	HOMEOSTASIS

ration and meaninglessness are actually statements of the *human condition*. Having and being are alternative ways of dealing with the pain associated with meaninglessness and separation. Each of the four states is defined briefly in this chapter, before being treated in more depth in chapters 2 through 5, respectively.

The life matrix is not a quick-fix panacea promising fame, fortune, love, and eternal bliss for those who use it. Rather it is a tool that many have found helpful, if properly used, in their search.

Life on the Island and Elsewhere

Is the meaning from the island what French writers Albert Camus and Jean-Paul Sartre would have us believe? Life is truly "absurd" and has no meaning at all? Nowhere is the case for *meaninglessness* expressed more eloquently and more forcefully than in the book of Ecclesiastes in the Bible:

> Our fate is like that of the animals; the same fate awaits us both; as one dies, so dies the other. All have the same breath; we have no advantage over the animals. Everything is meaningless. All go to the same place; all come from dust, and to dust all return.
>
> (3:19-20 NIV, adapted)

If one contemplates the grim history of Native Americans and African American slaves or the millions who lost their lives during Stalin's reign of terror, Hitler's Holocaust, or Mao's Cultural Revolution, one need not be a cynic to conclude that life is meaningless. The death of a child or a natural disaster such as a hurricane, a tornado, or an earthquake may also lead to Ecclesiastes' conclusion that everything is meaningless, "a chasing after the wind."

Only by coming to terms with one's own meaninglessness can one hope to find personal meaning as well as meaning in the family and in the workplace. Many have found that writing their own personal history is an effective way of differentiating between those events which are truly meaningful and those which are not.

The Meaninglessness of Old Age

$\mathcal{R}$emember your Creator
   in the days of your youth,
before the days of trouble come
   and the years approach when you will say,
   "I find no pleasure in them"—
before the sun and the light
   and the moon and the stars grow dark,
   and the clouds return after the rain;
when the keepers of the house tremble,
   and the strong men stoop,
when the grinders cease because they are few,
   and those looking through the windows grow dim;
when the doors to the street are closed
   and the sound of grinding fades;
when men rise up at the sound of birds,
   but all their songs grow faint;
when men are afraid of heights
   and of dangers in the streets;
when the almond tree blossoms
   and the grasshopper drags himself along
   and desire no longer is stirred.
Then man goes to his eternal home
   and mourners go about the streets.

Remember him—before the silver cord is severed,
   or the golden bowl is broken;
before the pitcher is shattered at the spring,
   or the wheel broken at the well,
and the dust returns to the ground it came from,
   and the spirit returns to God who gave it.

"Meaningless! Meaningless!" says the Teacher.
   "Everything is meaningless!"

ECCLESIASTES 12:1-8 NIV

Although life may be meaningful, meaning often eludes those on the island and elsewhere who are unable to connect with either their inner self, other people, or some source of grounding. Those who are not in touch with their feelings and do not know who they are often suffer from low self-esteem, anxiety, and even depression. They are easily influenced by their parents, their lovers, their children, and their friends. In addition, those who are separated from themselves are frequently lonely, paranoid, and afraid of dying. They are estranged from the soul that defines who they really are. *Separation* from oneself can be caused by inconsistent parental support, childhood abuse, sexual abuse, religious indoctrination, overindulgence in consumer goods, poverty, and homelessness.

A second form of separation stems from an inability to connect with other people, either through personal love relationships or through a genuine sense of community. Cathexis (attachment) with other human beings on a deserted island is clearly an impossible dream. Unrequited love and unfulfilled expectations for community can precipitate feelings of isolation and emptiness as well as spiritual detachment, alienation, anxiety, and hypochondria.

A third type of separation results from a lack of depth or grounding in one's life, leading also to alienation and detachment from one's sense of being. To deal with separation on the island, some say they would turn to God, nature, or possibly the animals.

In an attempt to avoid the pain and suffering associated with separation and meaninglessness both on the island and in the real world, many of us seek meaning through a life based on *having*. For those into having, life on the island may seem like paradise. You can truly have it all on the island. Everything there is yours. You are completely in charge. Since there is no government, there are no rules, no government regulations, no taxes, no special interest groups, and no welfare cheats. Poverty, homelessness, substance abuse, crime, and violence are completely unknown on the island.

By owning, manipulating, and controlling material possessions, wealth, and other people, we hope to find security and certainty in an otherwise uncertain world. We think we can consume our way into a state of never-ending self-actualization without paying any psychological dues for our life of unrestrained pleasure. Those in the having mode want to hold on to what they've got at any cost. They live by the slogan, "I've got mine, Jack." What life is all about is "looking out for number one."

In a parable, Jesus mocked the futility of the having mode of dealing with life's uncertainties:

> The land of a rich man brought forth plentifully; and he thought to himself, "What shall I do, for I have nowhere to store my crops?" And he said, "I will do this: I will pull down my barns, and build larger ones; and there I will store all my grain and my goods. And I will say to my soul, Soul, you have ample goods laid up for many years; take your ease, eat, drink, be merry." But God said to him, "Fool! This night your soul is required of you; and the things you have prepared, whose will they be?" So is he who lays up treasure for himself, and is not rich toward God. (Luke 12:16-21 RSV)

Legalism, religious orthodoxy, and political conservatism are often associated with a personal philosophy based on having. Judaism and Christianity are religions that stress adherence to norms. The rules of law and moral conduct associated with these respective religions are attributed to God. Religious norms, which are gifts to point the way to God, can become idolatrous, taking the place of God. Having always substitutes some thing—a possession, a rule, an idea—in the place of our insecurity before God. Political ideology, patriotism, and nationalism can be examples of legalism to support a life of having. Biblical religion has always thought of having as the inappropriate attempt of the creature to solve the problem of human vulnerability through attachment to things rather than God.

Economist Milton Friedman is the patron saint of those who are into having. His statement that "the only social responsibility of business is to make as much money as possible for the stockholders" attracted the enthusiastic support of the "me" generation, since its attachment to "me" leaves little room for concern for problems of moral or social responsibility. Businesspersons can do no wrong so long as it is legal and they are making as much money as possible for the shareholders.

Our love affair with the automobile is the quintessential example of the law of having. With the automobile one has the feeling of freedom, power, and control. If you have a Honda, you will soon have your eye on a BMW, which will only suffice until you can afford something even more pricey. Psychologists have long noted an ever-rising "threshold of expectation" in our materialism. The more you have, the more you want. Whether one is into having expensive homes, Persian rugs, priceless art objects, thoroughbred race horses, beautiful women, or political power, the story is the same. Having has no upper limits.

But as psychologist Erich Fromm has noted, having is an illusory source of meaning: "If I am what I have and if what I have is lost, who then am I?"[1] Or as Jesus said, "Fool! This night your soul is required of you; and the things you have prepared, whose will they be?" Such thoughts must have weighed heavily on the mind of publishing tycoon Robert Maxwell the night of his mysterious death alone on his private yacht off the Canary Islands—knowing that his publishing empire was on the brink of collapse. Financial high rollers Ivan Boesky, Michael Milken, and Donald Trump may have experienced similar feelings as their fortunes began unraveling.

> *M*oney is my first, last and only love.
>
> ARMAND HAMMER

In response to a "spiritual reawakening" triggered by disillusionment with his vast collection of worldly possessions, Thomas Monaghan, the wealthy founder of Domino's Pizza, suddenly began selling off many of his prized possessions, including three houses designed by Frank Lloyd Wright and thirty vintage automobiles, one of which was a $13 million Bugatti. Construction was halted on his new $5 million home, and he even sold his Detroit Tigers baseball team because it was a "source of excessive pride." He was quoted as saying, "None of the things I've bought, and I mean none of them, have ever really made me happy."[2] Ironically, some of the principal beneficiaries of our economic system—the super rich—become its biggest losers. They sometimes pay a huge spiritual, intellectual, and emotional price for their accumulation of material wealth. And what affects the spirit, has consequences for the body. A physician recently told us, "We once thought of heart disease as a male disease. Now we're seeing more heart ailments among women. I suppose this means that women are at last making it big in business."

Our entire economy is driven by our intense psychological need to fill a spiritual and emotional vacuum. If we are feeling down and need a lift, we buy a new dress, have lunch in a nice restaurant, or see a movie. A whole new cult of teenagers, known affectionately as "mall rats," has emerged in shopping malls throughout the country; they seem to live only to go to the mall. But material goods and services themselves produce more meaninglessness. It's a vicious circle. So important is meaninglessness to the economy that President Bush's seductive 1992 State of the Union message to a nation with one of the worst saving rates in the West was, "Buy now and save for retirement later." Apparently, if we don't play the game, the whole house of cards will come tumbling down. We have a patriotic duty to consume. Minneapolis now has the "Mall of America," which contains 2.5 million square feet of retail floor space. America has become a mall.

Many philosophers reject the idea of any form of cosmic meaning imposed on us by some external force such as God, Jesus, Buddha, Muhammad, nature, or the universe. In their view, if life has meaning, then we must create our own through *being* rather than *having*. Being involves loving, caring, sharing, cooperating, and participating in communities, in contrast to owning, manipulating, and controlling. According to Erich Fromm, the anxiety and insecurity engendered by the risk of losing what one has acquired is absent in the being mode. "If I am who I am and not what I have, nobody can deprive me of or threaten my security and my sense of identity."[3] Among the possible sources of meaning that can be realized only through being are:

1. *Our Creations*—what we accomplish or give back to the world through our creativity.
2. *Love Relationships*—what we give to and take from the

world through our encounters, experiences, and personal relationships.

3. *Community*—our integration into and participation in worthwhile groups.

4. *Pain, Suffering, and Death*—our stand toward a fate we cannot change.[4]

We alone create our own history, meaning, and eternity.

THE ECONOMIST

Obviously, human love and community are out of the question on a deserted island. However, it is possible to paint pictures on the walls of caves, build a house, write poetry, compose music, sing, and play a hand-crafted musical instrument. But would these creations provide meaning, if there were no one around with whom to share them?

In his provocative essay "The Power of the Powerless," former Czechoslovak President and playwright Vaclav Havel called for a revolution and "moral reconstitution of society":

A new experience of being, a renewed rootedness in the universe, a newly grasped sense of "higher responsibility," a new-found inner relationship to other people and to the human community—these factors clearly indicate the direction in which we must go.[5]

Many of the so-called pop psychology books of the 1980s claimed that meaning can be found only by turning inward. Although self-actualization may be a necessary condition for finding meaning, the deserted island suggests that it may not be sufficient. *Is it possible to be—without human love and community?* Doesn't the search for meaning involve reaching out to others as well as looking within yourself? In the words of theologian Paul Tillich, "Only in the continuous encounter with other persons does the person become and remain a person. The place of this encounter is the community."[6]

One of the toughest challenges we face in our search is how to balance the spiritual, emotional, intellectual, and physiological forces in our lives—each of which contributes to our sense of meaning. For our spiritual needs we can seek the help of a priest or a rabbi. A philosopher or a theologian may counsel us in our intellectual pursuits. A psychologist, a social worker, or a psychiatrist may provide psychotherapy to help heal our emotional wounds. And a physician may treat our physical ailments.

Unfortunately, the determinants of life's meaning are interdependent. Priests may know a lot about religion, theology, and philosophy but have limited knowledge of psychotherapy and medicine. Psychologists may be well grounded in psychotherapy but have little appreciation for the physiological origins of some mental illness. Ultimately, we cannot expect someone else to hand us meaning. Balance must come from our own integration of the forces of life. An important by-product of our search process is a set of guidelines for balancing the forces of meaning and integrating them into one's life.

The Process

If life does have meaning, it may very well lie in the search itself. Our search process consists of the following seven steps:

1. Review the most meaningful events in your *life history.*
2. Come to terms with the *meaninglessness* in your own life.
3. Confront your *separation* from yourself, others, and the ground of your being.
4. Contemplate the consequences of a life devoted to *having.*
5. Seek meaning through *being*—through your creations, love relationships, sense of community, and pain and suffering.
6. Formulate a *personal philosophy,* which addresses meaning, values, ethical principles, and social responsibility.
7. Formulate a *personal strategy,* which includes an external environmental forecast, a situation assessment, objectives, goals, and strategies.

An integral part of our search process involves the writing of a personal philosophy and a personal strategic plan (steps 6 and 7). A personal philosophy is a statement of the fundamental principles on which we base our lives. It attempts to capture our sense of meaning and direction and brings discipline to our search. A well-conceived philosophy will help shape our goals, objectives, and behavior. It is a mirror image of our heart and soul defining the essence of our existence, who we really are. Everyone has a philosophy. Few take the time to write theirs down. Our philosophy may also be used to devise a road map for our search. Just as corporate managers can find it useful to formulate a long-term business plan, we too may benefit from such a process in our personal lives—spiritually, emotionally, intellectually, physiologically, professionally, and financially.

---

*O*ur personal history, which has been strongly influenced by our environment—particularly our parents—cannot be rewritten. However, we acquire the power and the energy to shape our future and our eternity when we begin questioning the meaning of our life.

THE PSYCHIATRIST

We believe that meaning can be found by virtually anyone whether one be a believer or a nonbeliever, rich or poor, young or old, educated or uneducated. There are many paths to meaning, but few, if any, avoid confronting our need for human love and empathy and our intense longing for community. *Most combine a journey inward with an outward quest.*

What role, if any, can religion play in our search? Some view religion merely as a set of dogmas imposed on us during our childhood by the local minister, priest, or rabbi. Others equate religion with the fundamentalist message of television evangelists Pat Robertson, Jimmy Swaggart, and Jerry Falwell. Nothing could be farther from the truth. Religion is our way of dealing with the mysteries of life and death. It is an affirmation that we are not left entirely to our own devices in our search. The purpose of religion is to prepare us for death by teaching us how to live. Religion is fundamental to the search.

> $\mathcal{G}$od is our ultimate source of meaning. But who is God? That is *the* question.
>
> THE PASTOR

Both the existence and nature of God are shrouded in mystery. Human life is finite. If there is life after death, what do we know of it? Through the exercise of our personal freedom we confront not only our own death, but our own history, meaning, and eternity.

Ultimately, the search for meaning is concerned with planning the condition of our soul for the time of our death, when the spiritual, intellectual, emotional, and physiological dimensions of our life collapse into one. A facile humanism pales before the awesome finality of our death. What will be our enduring legacy on earth? What is the essence of our lives? We must prepare ourselves for this final accounting through the never-ending search, always pushing our knowledge of life and death to the limit, always wrestling meaning out of meaninglessness.

We now turn to a more detailed discussion of meaninglessness, separation, having, and being.

Chapter 2

MEANINGLESSNESS

Mother died today. Or, maybe, yesterday; I can't be sure. The telegram from the Home says: YOUR MOTHER PASSED AWAY. FUNERAL TOMORROW. DEEP SYMPATHY. Which leaves the matter doubtful; it could have been yesterday.

ALBERT CAMUS
THE STRANGER

Le Malaise

Jan and Justin

Jan is an attractive, intelligent thirty-five-year-old socialite living in Richmond, Virginia's upscale West End. A graduate of a fashionable Virginia women's college, Jan is the mother of seven-year-old Kim and ten-year-old Ashley. Both Jan and her husband, Justin, come from old line Richmond families and went to the most exclusive private school in the city. Kim and Ashley attend the same school. Justin is a prominent attorney who is active in state politics.

Jan abandoned her plans to become an investigative reporter when Ashley was born and has never been employed outside the home—a subject about which she is quite sensitive. Life for Jan is entirely centered on Kim and Ashley and the chic Country Club of Virginia social scene. Her typical day includes tennis and lunch at the club, driving Ashley to ballet classes, picking up Kim after school, and shopping at the neighborhood food market. Life often seems to be little more than one continuous car pool.

Jan's well-appointed home contains virtually every known high-tech labor-saving device. The home computer is even used to schedule car pools and tennis matches. The family seldom denies itself material possessions, for which it has an insatiable appetite. Jan and the girls often spend weekends in their cottage on the river. In the summer they go to Bald Head Island in North Carolina.

Although Jan was brought up as a United Methodist, she drifted away from the church in the 1980s—partly in response to her sense of outrage over the religious fundamentalism espoused by TV evangelists Jim and Tammy Bakker, Jimmy Swaggart, and Jerry Falwell. Not unlike many of her contemporaries, Jan equates religion with Protestant fundamentalism. She feels strongly that a woman should have the right to choose whether or not she has an abortion. Once or twice a year she attends services at an Episcopal church conveniently located across the street from the country club.

Jan has few interests beyond her family and the small group of women with whom she plays tennis. Some nights when she is unable to sleep, she occasionally lies awake and wonders, Is there nothing more to life than tennis and car pools? Unfortunately, these feelings do not lead to any action or changes in her behavior. She does not have time to read the daily newspaper even though she once aspired to be a journalist. She rarely watches the evening news on TV and does not participate in community activities. For all practical purposes she is completely disengaged from her neighbors, her city, her state, her nation, and the rest of the world. She lives only for herself and her family.

Although Justin is seldom at home in the evening, Jan and Justin do occasionally entertain his clients and friends in their home. Justin still smokes and is a heavy drinker. He is not very close to Kim or Ashley—or Jan, for that matter. Jan suspected that he was having an affair with his secretary in his law firm's downtown apartment. One evening she decided to check up on him and arrived unannounced at the apartment where she found him in bed with Stephanie.

Angry, depressed, and suicidal, Jan turned to a psychiatrist to help her confront her malaise—the meaninglessness and emptiness of her life.

Marilene and Laszlo

Even more desperate than Jan was Marilene, a beautiful Hungarian woman who taught psychology in a small college in the San

Francisco Bay area. Marilene, her husband Laszlo, and their daughter, Maria, immigrated to the United States from Hungary after the Communist government in Budapest dissolved in 1989. Laszlo Kovacs had been a senior intelligence officer in the Foreign Ministry of the Communist government.

For more than fifteen years, Marilene and Laszlo had enjoyed the privileges of the Party elites in Budapest. With the demise of communism, their whole world had collapsed—their ideology, their political influence, and their financial security. Laszlo was teaching international relations in a major university just outside San Francisco. This provided a convenient form of denial of the contradiction between his new life in capitalist America compared with his previous life under Hungarian socialism.

Marilene, Laszlo, and their daughter lived the life of a typical American yuppie family. They restored an old house in San Francisco and furnished it with all the right things. Laszlo drove a BMW and Marilene a Saab. They spent summer vacations at Pebble Beach, skied in Aspen over the Christmas holidays, and went to Lake Tahoe for spring break.

For nearly three years, life in the United States was a nonstop adventure for the Kovacs family. But gradually they began to realize that San Francisco was not Budapest and that never again would they experience the power, prestige, and level of affluence they had once enjoyed in Hungary. Their daughter began asking her father some very tough questions about his previous involvement with the Hungarian Communist Party. "How could you work for such a corrupt and incompetent regime?" she asked. In response to these questions as well as some of his own, Laszlo became depressed and started to drink. The existential crisis precipitated by his abrupt transition from the seat of Communist power to bourgeois capitalism was more than his soul could bear.

At the beginning of their fourth year in San Francisco, Marilene was swept off her feet by a self-proclaimed Bavarian count and multimillionaire, Ludwig Von Canon. Ludwig was an unscrupulous businessman who had amassed a huge fortune speculating in fake art and California real estate. He lived alone with his priceless pre-Columbian art collection in Sausalito overlooking San Francisco Bay.

Shortly thereafter, Marilene abruptly left her family, hoping to live with Ludwig. There was only one catch. Ludwig had another girlfriend, Sonya, with whom he had been romantically involved for over five years. Sonya ran a small art gallery in Sausalito, which served as a front for Ludwig's illicit art business. She was also a source of contacts for Von Canon's shady real estate ventures.

Ludwig was well connected to the San Francisco social scene and frequently invited Marilene to parties hosted by the rich and famous. Soon after Marilene left Laszlo, she became pregnant by Ludwig.

Several months later Ludwig was found dead on his couch in his Sausalito apartment. What initially appeared to be a suicide turned out not to be a suicide at all. Ludwig had been murdered by Sonya.

Sonya was convicted of second-degree murder and is serving time in a California state penitentiary. When Marilene's baby was born, Marilene, her daughter, and the baby moved to Vienna.

Communism, capitalism, jealousy, greed, lust, motherhood, and murder—what do they all mean? Maybe nothing.

Shakespeare on Meaninglessness

*T*omorrow, and tomorrow, and tomorrow,
Creeps in this petty pace from day to day,
To the last syllable of recorded time,
And all our yesterdays have lighted fools
The way to dusty death. Out, out, brief candle!
Life's but a walking shadow, a poor player
That struts and frets his hour upon the stage,
And then is heard no more: it is a tale
Told by an idiot, full of sound and fury,
Signifying nothing.

Macbeth, act 5, scene 4

Nothingness

The Los Angeles riots, racism, the bombing of the New York World Trade Center, the Iran-Contra affair, Colombian drug trafficking, Third World famines, the Balkan war, anarchy in former Soviet republics, and environmental pollution are all evidence of a world engulfed in meaninglessness. We have no sense of connectedness to ourselves, to others, to nature, to our history, or to the ground of our being. Our lives lack purpose and are grounded in nothingness.

Within a few hours after an all white Simi valley jury acquitted four policemen of the use of excessive force in the widely publicized videotape arrest and beating of Rodney King, South-central Los Angeles was ablaze. The two-day riot left 53 persons dead, injured 2,300, and resulted in the arrest of more than 10,000. Ten thousand buildings were either damaged or destroyed by fire and looting. More than 40,000 people lost their jobs, thousands were left homeless, and property damage alone was estimated to be well in excess of $1 billion.

Political pundits were quick to blame almost everyone for what happened in Los Angeles—white racists, black racists, Koreans, Rodney King, the jury, the L.A. mayor, the police chief, Lyndon Johnson, George Bush, black killer-rapist Willie Horton, liberals, conservatives, and the media, to mention only a few. Others pointed to capitalism, social welfare programs, teenage mothers, food stamps, rap music, and television violence. Nobody considered meaninglessness as the underlying cause of the violence—the meaningless life of alcohol abuser Rodney King, the policemen who beat him up, the policemen who stood by watching, the jury that acquitted him, impoverished African Americans living in Los Angeles, alienated whites, and opportunistic politicians.

What happened in Los Angeles could easily happen in dozens of other large cities throughout the United States. What was the purpose of the rioting? Did it have any meaning? What have we learned from the experience? Probably nothing. Meaninglessness breeds meaninglessness, and the cycle of narcissism and irresponsibility goes on and on.

Senator Bradley on Meaninglessness

*U*rban America has a crisis of meaning. Without meaning there can be no hope; without hope there can be no struggle; without struggle there can be no personal betterment. Absence of meaning, influenced by overt and subtle attacks from racist quarters over many years, as well as increasing pessimism about the possibility of justice, fosters a context for chaos and irresponsibility. Meaning develops from birth. Yet, more than forty percent of all births in the twenty largest cities of America are to women living alone; among Black women, more than sixty-five percent.

For kids who have no family outside the gang, no connection to religion, no sense of place outside the territory, and no imagination beyond the violence on TV, our claims that government is on their side ring hollow. To them, government is at best, incompetent, and at worst corrupt. Instead of being rooted in values such as commitment and community service, their desires, like commodities, become rooted in the shallow ground of immediate gratification. TV bombards these kids with messages of conspicuous consumption. They want it now. They become trapped in the quick-sands of American materialism, surfeited with images of sex, violence, and drugs.

The physical condition of American cities, in the absence of meaning in more and more lives, comes together at the barrel of a gun. If you were to select one thing that has changed in cities since the 1970s, it would be fear. Fear covers the streets like a sheet of ice. The number of murders and violent crimes has doubled in the twenty largest cities since 1978. Ninety percent of all violence is committed by males, and they are its predominant victims. Indeed, murder is the leading cause of death among young Black males.

SENATOR BILL BRADLEY
speech delivered one month before the Rodney King verdict

When Hurricane Andrew slammed into South Miami in August 1992 with its 160 mph winds, 63,000 homes were destroyed and 250,000 people were left homeless. Property damage was estimated to be between $15 and $20 billion. What do we make of such massive destruction? What possible meaning could it have? Is the meaning of Andrew that life has no meaning?

One of us recently visited several community development projects supported by the Christian Children's Fund in Guatemala. Included in the visit was the Nueva Vida project situated in the midst of a highly concentrated barrio located only a few blocks from one of the most posh neighborhoods in Guatemala City. Several thousand people in this area live in a complex maze of single-room, rodent-infested, dirt-floor shacks with wood stoves and no plumbing. Chickens, pigs, dogs, and cats roam freely among dark, filthy shacks, some of which are inhabited by as many as a dozen people. One could only imagine what life must be like in these miserable hovels during the rainy season.

In one shack were three small boys—beautiful beyond words—confined to a three-foot-square chicken-wire cage on the dirt floor. The haunting memory of their smiling faces will not soon be forgotten. The cage was in fact their baby-sitter—far better to be encaged in a chicken coop than to roam the streets of Guatemala City where children simply disappear. In a Guatemalan newspaper, the photographs and biographical sketches of three missing children alongside a one-page McDonald's advertisement promoting "Pollo McFrito" said it all. If life has meaning, how can such intense misery exist in the backyards of the super rich?

For forty-five years our nation was obsessed with the injustice of Communist governments in Eastern Europe and the Soviet Union. Yet nowhere in Eastern Europe and the former Soviet republics in recent times did one find political and economic repression comparable to what exists today in Guatemala. In addition to the risks of devastating earthquakes, active volcanoes, and perennial droughts, Guatemalans are subjected to never-ending civil violence and immeasurable poverty.

Consider the case of the Mayan village Santa Maria de Jesus, adjacent two volcanoes and located off a dirt road forty-five minutes from Antigua. With a population of 7,000, Santa Maria has no indigenous source of water whatsoever and is literally covered with volcanic dust. The village at one time received water from neighboring villages through two pipelines. Unfortunately, the mayor of Santa Maria sold one of the pipelines to another village and the second pipeline source dried up. Water is now bused from Antigua daily. Each family is entitled to one jug of water every three days to meet all of its needs.

Behind sandbags on every street corner of Santa Maria stood a teenage soldier armed with an automatic rifle. Many of these recruits were kidnapped by the military from other villages and forced into the killing business. There were fifty soldiers stationed throughout the village, where they had been since the village was invaded by a small band of guerrillas a year earlier. The military had countered with nearly a thousand troops flown in by helicopter. Half a dozen villagers, including two children, were killed in the cross fire.

Since the late 1970s, tens of thousands of Guatemalans have lost their lives in the war between the guerrillas and the military for the control of the rural villages. More than 250,000 children have been displaced as a result of the fighting—many of whom are now orphans. Of children under the age of five, 45 percent show signs of severe mental, physical, and growth retardation. Many important lakes and streams have tested positive for the cholera bacterium. Seventy percent of the population of 9.2 million is illiterate, and 2.3 million rural children have no educational opportunities whatsoever.

How can our own lives ever be complete and meaningful so long as the children of Guatemala, Haiti, Peru, Bangladesh, Ethiopia, Mozambique, Somalia, Sudan, and a dozen or so other similar countries are allowed to endure such enormous pain and suffering? Our smug self-satisfaction with our lives in the affluent West is testimony to our utter disregard of the fate of countless children in poorer countries. "Meaningless! Meaningless!" said the teacher in Ecclesiastes. "Everything is meaningless!"

Meaninglessness looms even larger when we review the forty-five-year history of the cold war between the United States and the

Soviet Union. Between 1945 and 1990, the United States spent more than $11 trillion on the cold war. During this period there were more than 1,900 nuclear explosions worldwide following Hiroshima and Nagasaki—equivalent to one explosion every nine days. The United States exploded more than 950 nuclear weapons while the Soviet Union exploded more than 700.

If we are serious about our quest for meaning, then we must confront head-on the very real possibility illustrated by some of the examples in this chapter that life is indeed absurd and has no meaning whatsoever. Maybe the story of the deserted island—not unlike life on the planet Earth—is a story about meaninglessness. In the words of Jean-Paul Sartre, "It is meaningless that we are born; it is meaningless that we die."[1] Not only is there no grand design for life, but there are no guidelines for living other than those which we create for ourselves. As Albert Camus said in *The Rebel:*

> If we believe in nothing, if nothing has any meaning and if we can affirm no values whatsoever, then everything is possible and nothing has any importance. There is no pro or con: the murderer is neither right nor wrong. We are free to stoke the crematory fires or to devote ourselves to the care of lepers. Evil and virtue are mere chance or caprice.[2]

What are some of the consequences of meaninglessness for life itself? Is survival possible in a world without meaning? The first column of the life matrix described in chapter 1 depicts some of the spiritual, intellectual, emotional, and physiological effects of meaninglessness.

If life is indeed absurd and it means absolutely nothing to live or die or to be a human being, then where else can life lead other than to spiritual emptiness and despair? Homicide, suicide, infanticide, matricide, patricide, fratricide, and genocide are all acts of nihilism.

The price of meaninglessness is nothingness, which is more than most souls can tolerate. Spiritual emptiness is a precursor of hopelessness, depression, existential sickness, and eventually physical death. For many people, confinement on the deserted island would be tantamount to death.

Despair

$\mathcal{D}$espair is the price one pays for self-awareness. Look deeply into life, and you will always find despair.[3]

IRVIN D. YALOM
When Nietzsche Wept

What about those who are physically or mentally challenged, such as the blind, the deaf, the mute, the paraplegic, or those suffering from cerebral palsy or Down syndrome? Are these conditions permanent impediments to the search for meaning, or can they actually become sources of meaning for both the victims as well as their families and loved ones? What meaning is there to the life of a person lying comatose in a hospital bed for months or even years sustained only by high-tech respirators and sophisticated microprocessors? And what of the "living dead"? Have they not confined themselves to their own deserted island? There is no escape from the island. The island is everywhere.

Groundhog Day, a popular movie starring Bill Murray, depicts the meaningless life of a Pittsburgh TV weatherman who finds himself doomed to relive the same day over and over again. Everyday is Groundhog Day, and there literally is no tomorrow. In response to his plight—or perhaps what is the cause of it—Murray eats too much, drinks too much, and sleeps around too much. He even tries unsuccessfully to commit suicide a few times, only to wake up the next morning and have it be February 2 again.

Effects of Meaninglessness

Spiritual ———————▶ Despair
Intellectual ———————▶ Nihilism
Emotional ———————▶ Depression
Physiological ———————▶ Death

Some Christians incorrectly associate atheism and agnosticism with meaninglessness and despair. This is unfair. Although atheists do not believe in a cosmic source of meaning originating outside the human psyche, it is possible for an atheist to enjoy a well-defined secular sense of meaning. Just as Christians, Jews, and other believers in God may experience spiritual growth and an integrated life, so too may atheists and agnostics. Even though believers may question the sufficiency of an atheist's system of meaning, monotheists do not have a monopoly on meaning.

Unless we come to terms with *nihilism*—absolute meaninglessness—we are likely to be drawn to superficial, inadequate sources of meaning simply because they promise to curb the pain and anxiety associated with the search—a promise not likely to be realized. For example, the biblical books Ecclesiastes and Job—required reading for all who are involved in the search—very effectively use nihilism to dramatize the question, What is life really all about?

German philosopher Friedrich Nietzsche and French existentialists Albert Camus and Jean-Paul Sartre each used the hopelessness and despair of nihilism to energize their quest for life's meaning. After asserting that life is absurd, since it is void of any cosmic source of meaning, Camus then proceeded to sketch out the elements of a humanistic philosophy of life consisting of values, ethics, and social responsibility. Nowhere to be found in Camus's writings is a succinct summary of the meaning of life. Rather what one does find is a collection of well-articulated, poignant themes about life, love, meaning, happiness, and death.

In one of his "Letters to a German Friend," Camus said,

> I continue to believe that this world has no ultimate meaning. But I know that something in it has a meaning and that is man, because he is the only creature to insist on having one. This world has at least the truth of man, and our task is to provide its justifications against fate itself. And it has no justification but man; hence he must be saved if we want to save the idea we have of life.[4]

But in the preface to *The Myth of Sisyphus*, Camus laid the groundwork for an ethical theory of value-nihilism: "Within the limits of nihilism it is possible to find the means to proceed beyond nihil-ism."[5]

Job on Meaninglessness

*L*et the day perish in which I was born,
    and the night that said,
    "A man-child is conceived."
Let that day be darkness!
    May God above not seek it,
    or light shine on it.
Let gloom and deep darkness claim it.
    Let clouds settle upon it;
    let the blackness of the day terrify it.
. . . .

Why did I not die at birth,
    come forth from the womb and expire?
Why were there knees to receive me,
    or breasts for me to suck?
Now I would be lying down and quiet;
    I would be asleep; then I would be at rest
with kings and counselors of the earth
    who rebuild ruins for themselves,
or with princes who have gold,
    who fill their houses with silver.
Or why was I not buried like a stillborn child,
    like an infant that never sees the light?
There the wicked cease from troubling,
    and there the weary are at rest.
There the prisoners are at ease together;
    they do not hear the voice of the taskmaster.
The small and the great are there,
    and the slaves are free from their masters.
Why is light given to one in misery,
    and life to the bitter in soul?

Job 3:3-5, 11-20

The overriding concern of Camus in most of his work was expressed by Caligula, the hero in Camus's play bearing the same name, "Men die; and they are not happy."[6] Beginning with his first novel *A Happy Death,* which was not published until after his death in an automobile accident in 1960, Camus returned over and over again to the theme that the purpose of life is not to be happy, as the "me" generation would have us believe, but rather *to die happy.* In Camus's novel *The Stranger,* as well as his four plays *Caligula, The Misunderstanding, State of Siege,* and *The Just Assassins,* the theme was always the same—die happy.

> *Is* it possible that the absurd is a metaphor for God? Or is God a metaphor for the absurd?
>
> THE ECONOMIST

But if one expects to die happy, then one must begin a pilgrimage which ultimately ends in a happy death. Above all, there is "a will to live without rejecting anything of life, which is the virtue I honor most in this world."[7] Not surprisingly, Camus rejected murder, suicide, and the state-imposed death penalty. His sense of personal meaning and values gave high priority to courage, pride, love, community, and social justice. In addition, Camus felt strong affinity with the poor and underprivileged in society.

It was hardly surprising that Camus's philosophy was not widely acclaimed by the academic establishment. Camus managed to figure out all too many pieces of life's puzzle—meaninglessness, celebration of life, living with what you know, soul crafting, and happy death. Many of his ideas were very threatening to the conventional wisdom. A philosophy which declares that people should be judged by who they are and what they do rather than by what they own or control was guaranteed to encounter rough sledding in our consumer-oriented, materialistic society.

The denial of meaninglessness in our own lives helps explain the separation and alienation experienced by many of us as well as our irresistible attraction to a life based on having. Rather than deal with the frightening specter of nihilism and all its pain and uncertainty, we try to escape through narcissism, hedonism, consumerism, and simplistic religious dogmas and political ideologies, both liberal and conservative. A firm grasp of nihilism and all its implications is absolutely essential to the search for meaning. There is no escape from the possibility of nothingness.

Albert Einstein once said, "The man who regards his own life and that of his fellow creatures as meaningless is not merely unhappy but hardly fit for life."[8] The debilitating emotional effects of meaninglessness are well known—anxiety, depression, and the possibility of complete emotional collapse. There are no limits on the extremes to which people will go to avoid the emotional pain of meaninglessness. Some try to find meaning through their children, their jobs, sexual abuse, alcoholism, drugs, political ideology, racial prejudice, or violence. Others turn to technological gimmicks such as personal computers, VCRs, video games, and mobile telephones.

The increased use of medication by psychiatrists is hardly surprising in an era of instant gratification in which patients are looking for quick relief from their existential pain. Although neuroleptic drugs and antidepressants may provide temporary solace from the fear of meaninglessness, there is no substitute for the unremitting search.

In addition to the adverse spiritual, intellectual, and emotional effects of meaninglessness, there are often physiological effects as well. One need not be a mystic to recognize that one's physical well-being is often influenced by one's emotional state. Our will to live and our desire to recover from illness are closely linked to our sense of meaning. Meaninglessness and despair are not conducive to a long and healthy life.

The decision to take one's own life is the ultimate form of nihilism. Many Americans were surprised to learn that a book advising terminally ill people how to commit suicide surged to the top of the *New York Times* best-seller list the very first week it was in print. The book *Final Exit* was written by Derek Humphry, executive director of the Hemlock Society, an organization that provides advice on how to commit suicide.

Just as active participation in the death of a human being through suicide, abortion, self-defense, or murder may be a statement of life's meaninglessness, so too is passive approval of state-sponsored executions, wars, and military adventures. To kill a human being (including oneself) is to deny the possibility that the life of that person may have meaning. By whose authority other than the law of the jungle do those who kill or sanction killing set themselves up as both judge and executioner?

Wars and executions in the name of the state occur when our sense of community gives way to our pagan lust for revenge—a lust firmly grounded in nihilism. Violence begets more violence, not the other way around.

Although a woman has the right to decide whether or not she has an abortion, the decision to abort a fetus is a very strong declaration of the meaning of life, not just a quick fix for a personal problem. Nor is the father of an unborn child absolved of responsibility in the decision to abort the fetus, even if he openly objects to the mother's decision. The time to discuss the meaning of the life of a fetus is before sexual intercourse, not after the fetus is a fait accompli. One of the leading reasons for sexual promiscuity is that many feel they are worthless unless they are of use to or are using another for pleasure.

Many high-tech medical procedures such as amniocentesis raise fundamental questions about the meaning of life. Amniocentesis is a highly intrusive test which has gained widespread acceptance among affluent older pregnant women in America. By taking a sample of the amniotic fluid from the embryo sac of the mother, it is possible to analyze the chromosome structure of the fetus so as to detect anomalies such as Down syndrome. If the mother or the parents do not like the results of the test, they can ask the physician to abort the fetus. However, amniocentesis is not a risk-free procedure. There is significant risk of either injury to the fetus by the needle used to collect the fluid or infection to the mother.

Contrary to the way in which amniocentesis is often represented by obstetricians, it is not a value-neutral scientific panacea. Unless parents are willing to subject a fetus to the risk of unintended fatal injury or are willing to take the life of the unborn baby through abortion because of chromosomal anomalies, then amniocentesis introduces more moral and ethical questions than it answers.

At the heart of the debate over euthanasia and when to pull the plug on the life support systems of a terminally ill patient are questions related to the meaning of the patient's life. Does the life of an unconscious terminally ill patient have any meaning? Who is qualified to answer this complex question? The patient's physician, spouse, family, friends, priest, or rabbi?

Behind many of our expenditures for medical research, behind our quest for painless existence, "safe sex," simple solutions, and morally neutral procedures is our desire for instant gratification—avoidance of the search.

Where Is the Glue?

For more than seventy years, Marxist-Leninist ideology provided the spiritual glue that held the Soviet Union together. Although Stalinist communism was completely discredited by former Soviet leader Mikhail S. Gorbachev, it has not been replaced by a meaningful vision of the future other than American-style consumerism, which is vacuous. This lack of spiritual glue not only resulted in the collapse of the Soviet Union, but contributed to the political instability which pervades Eastern Europe. Today, in every Eastern European country and former Soviet republic, there is some form of deep-rooted ethnic, religious, or nationalistic turmoil.

Held together for decades by the iron fist of its Communist dictator Tito, Yugoslavia has come unglued at the seams. The conflict between Serbia and Croatia and Bosnia and Herzegovina is as old as the feuds between Eastern Orthodox believers and Roman Catholics and Muslims respectively. We see little evidence to suggest that the bloody Balkan experience will not be replicated all over Eastern Europe and throughout the former Soviet republics.

Three years after it gained its freedom from Moscow, Czechoslovakia split—nonviolently—into two independent nations. Although Hungary had a thirty-year head start over its other Eastern European neighbors in introducing economic and political reforms, it is not without its own political problems. Hungary has nearly fifty political parties and it does not get along with its Serbian and Rumanian neighbors. Rumania, the most repressive of the former Soviet Eastern European allies, still has a long way to go before becoming a democracy. Many Rumanians harbor strong negative feeling toward the 2 million ethnic Hungarians living in Transylvania. There is also considerable tension between Rumania and Moldova. The Bulgarians viewed the Soviets as their liberators, because the Russians freed them from the Ottoman Turks in 1877. Today there is still no love lost between the Bulgarians and the Turks.

The Poles are still reeling from the political and economic effects of the so-called shock therapy approach to crash capitalism embraced by the Polish government. Although shops are full of food and other consumer goods, prices are so high that few Poles can afford to purchase what is available. As inefficient, state-owned enterprises were shut down, unemployment soared and income plummeted. Crime and corruption increased dramatically. Warsaw is now the stolen-car capital of Europe. There is constant squabbling among the several dozen political parties over the future direction of Poland, about which there is no consensus. Although Poland will probably survive the transition to a market economy, it may not be out of the woods yet.

Of the former Eastern European Communist countries, only East Germany was thought to be relatively secure politically and economically, as a result of its acquisition by West Germany. However, the high cost of the merger precipitated a strong recession and high unemployment in Germany, leading to increased anti-Semitism, Gypsy-bashing, and right-wing extremism.

Many of the fifteen former Soviet republics are on the brink of economic collapse and political anarchy. So severe is the spiritual and ideological crisis facing Eastern Europe and the former Soviet republics that many of these newly independent nations could soon find that they have merely traded in their old Communist dictator for a fascist tyrant disguised as a democrat.

Throughout the former Soviet republics, crime, corruption, substance abuse, prostitution, and smuggling are on the rise. Bribery has become a way of life. There is an anything goes attitude and a complete breakdown of discipline and trust. People are looking out only for themselves. What is sadly lacking is a well-defined sense of purpose or meaning. There are no quick-fix solutions to the problem of meaninglessness. Democracy and free markets alone will not fill the void left by the collapse of communism. None of the leaders of these emerging new nations is addressing the spiritual, emotional, and intellectual needs of a region consumed by turmoil. Where is the glue holding the former Soviet republics and Eastern European countries together? There is none!

But what about the United States? Where is the glue that binds our fifty states together? Throughout the twentieth century, four principal threats have helped keep our nation intact—World War I, the Great Depression, World War II, and the Soviet Union. However, for more than forty-five years our national sense of meaning was based almost entirely on anticommunism. This was particularly true during the McCarthy era of the 1950s and true as well in the Reagan years.

President Ronald Reagan was driven to show that literally everything the Soviets did was suspect and that no part of the Soviet arms buildup in the 1970s and 1980s was in response to American arms building or to the Soviets' perceptions of U.S. motives. According to this view, the only way to end the arms race was for the United States to press the Soviets to the wall and force them to back down. With this zero-sum mind-set, diplomatic negotiations were perceived to have little value. Everything that was true and good was on our side, and the Soviets were to blame for everything that went wrong. Simplistic though it was, the American people were mesmerized by this view of the Soviet Union throughout the 1980s. It was precisely what they wanted to hear and to believe.

During the cold war, we all knew exactly what we were against—Godless communism and the Soviet Union. But now that the cold war is finally over, we don't seem to have a clue as to what we are for.

The made-for-television Persian Gulf drama aimed squarely at the "living dead" and, precipitated by Saddam Hussein's invasion of Kuwait, contained all the essential ingredients for a Tom Clancy post–cold war thriller—a demonic enemy, suspense, political intrigue, high-tech military heroics, and Middle East oil. The action-packed TV series became an instantaneous success with American viewers in need of a new demon to replace the Soviet Union.

President George Bush had no difficulty convincing a receptive American TV audience that Saddam Hussein—a tyrant he helped create—was indeed the new Adolf Hitler.

At the apex of Soviet political power, it's hard to imagine Communist propaganda ever being as effective as that of the American television networks in supporting President Bush's military policies in the Persian Gulf. For weeks CNN provided its American viewers live twenty-four-hour coverage of the Middle East equivalent of "cowboys and indians." Americans were captivated by the one-sided, high-tech, patriotic hype. During the 1980s President Ronald Reagan was often shown on TV riding his horse on his ranch in California. To add drama to the Persian Gulf saga, Bush appeared frequently on TV making shoot-from-the-hip attacks on Saddam Hussein from his electric golf cart and his speedboat in Kennebunkport, Maine.

Although the cold war is finally over, our need for a bigger-than-life enemy seems never to end. At least for a while, Saddam Hussein was willing to fill this void. He played his role very well. Who will be the demon in Tom Clancy's next novel? Only time will tell.

Not unlike Brazil, China, India, and the former Soviet Union, the United States is fundamentally unmanageable in its present form. Just as Mr. Gorbachev found it impossible to manage the Soviet Union from Moscow, so too have the White House and the Congress found it equally futile to try to impose top-down Washington-based solutions on such problems as poverty, homelessness, racism, drug abuse, violent crime, child abuse, and a badly failing education system. The problems of the poor, the underprivileged, and the disfranchised are not susceptible to solutions imposed from above. Solutions require the bottom-up participation of those affected, as well as a sense of community that connects those who have been victimized with those in a position to influence the results.

The meaninglessness which abounds in the United States goes hand in glove with the absence of a sense of community one finds in our nation. Rarely do our schools, religious congregations, or places of employment encourage the search for meaning and community.

Regrettably, our nihilistic lack of meaning leads us to find an enemy to provide us the "glue" to hold our nation together. It is a sad testimonial to any society that the common fear of an alleged "enemy" is the only glue strong enough to hold it together.

Beyond Meaninglessness

Contrary to some of the grim examples contained in this chapter, meaninglessness need not necessarily be viewed as all gloom and doom. We believe that meaninglessness and death are two of the three most significant forces driving our search for meaning—the other being separation, which is the subject of chapter 3.

Only by confronting meaninglessness and our own mortality are we then prepared to embark on our pilgrimage. Just as a recovering alcoholic must come to terms with his or her powerlessness, so too must we confront the possibility that life is absurd and that we are going to die.

---

*H*ello darkness, my old friend
I've come to talk with you again.

PAUL SIMON
"The Sounds of Silence"

Once we have hit rock bottom, we may be more receptive to the challenge and the responsibility of creating our own meaning. Having encountered the stark nakedness of meaninglessness and the realization that there truly is "no such thing as a free lunch," we may then be catapulted kicking and screaming into the quest.

Once we realize the importance of meaninglessness in our search, we become less afraid of it. It somehow seems less awesome. Without meaninglessness and death staring us in the face, most of us would be complacent and lethargic. The living dead syndrome spoken of earlier is a reflection of our lack of courage in dealing with meaninglessness.

The threat of nothingness compels us to make something of our lives. Our only possible escape from the pangs of nihilism is by creating our own meaning, and we do so by the care and nurturing of our soul.

Chapter 3

SEPARATION

Separation is threefold: there is separation among individual lives, separation of a man from himself, and separation of all men from the Ground of Being.

PAUL TILLICH
THE SHAKING OF THE FOUNDATIONS

The Story of Johnny and Sasha

Johnny and Sasha are two blue-collar workers in their early twenties.[1] Johnny works in a General Motors plant near Detroit, and Sasha works for the St. Petersburg Shipyard (formerly the Leningrad Shipyard) in Russia.

Johnny's grandfather also worked for GM and recently retired after forty years on the assembly line. Having grown up in the rural South during the depression, he and his family experienced real poverty during the 1930s. He quit school when he was sixteen years old to help support the family, but later volunteered for the infantry in World War II.

After the war, Johnny's grandfather moved to Detroit where GM was hiring thousands of unskilled workers to meet the post-war demand for automobiles. His primary aim was to find a stable, secure job to support his family. He remembered the tough times of the 1930s all too well. For forty years he worked on one repetitive job after another—always doing what he had been told to do and never questioning the authority of his managers.

Sasha's grandfather barely survived the siege of Leningrad while serving in the Russian Army during the Great Patriotic War. Not only did he almost starve to death during the war, but he and his family experienced Stalin's reign of terror in the 1930s at very close range. Sasha's grandfather was not a risk-taker and had a healthy respect for military authority. After the war he was assigned a job at the shipyard where he worked until 1987.

Throughout the 1950s and 1960s, the hierarchical, authoritarian style of management of GM and the Leningrad Shipyard worked very well. The GM plant where Johnny's grandfather worked was one of the most efficient in the United States. The Leningrad Shipyard produced large tankers and cargo ships for the Soviet commercial fleet. In each case the workers and managers alike were poorly educated, had grown up in poverty, and had no problem whatsoever in working under regimented conditions.

When Johnny and Sasha were born, the standard of living in their respective families had improved appreciably since the end of the war. Although Johnny's family was better off than Sasha's, materially speaking, they both enjoyed a relatively comfortable standard of living.

Neither Johnny nor Sasha has ever experienced poverty. They both graduated from high school, took some additional college-level courses, grew up in a middle-class environment, and watched too much television. Johnny has never been exposed to military service. Although Sasha fulfilled his two-year Soviet military obligation, he hated every minute of it and strongly opposed the war in Afghanistan.

Johnny and Sasha are paid well, but their work is monotonous and unchallenging. They often wonder why a high school degree was required for such mindless jobs. Both Johnny and Sasha are grossly overqualified for their jobs.

Johnny is not interested in politics and has never registered to vote. Sasha is also apolitical and unlike his father and his grandfather did not join the Communist Party before its collapse in 1991.

Neither Johnny nor Sasha likes to work very hard. Given a choice between more work for more pay and a day off from work, they will always opt for the latter. Both Johnny and Sasha resent the heavy-handed, top-down, authoritarian style of management practiced by their respective employers. They are often late to work and frequently do not show up for work at all. Johnny smokes pot on the job and Sasha has a drinking problem. Sasha is still single, but Johnny is divorced.

The story of Johnny and Sasha is a story about the dehumanizing aspects of large industrial companies in the United States and Russia. Both Johnny's grandfather and Sasha's endured boring, repetitive, and sometimes dangerous jobs for four decades based on ignorance and fear. But the same working conditions in the 1990s produce feelings of alienation, detachment, ambivalence, and complete disaffection—feelings widespread throughout the industrial world.

Johnny and Sasha are alienated from their work, their supervisors, and their coworkers. They don't like their jobs, their bosses, their government, or themselves.

Most American and Russian companies employ the same management philosophy and organizational structures today that worked so well for them in the 1950s and 1960s. However, the typical worker in the 1950s was a child of poverty, uneducated, and comfortable with military authority. Today's workers in both countries are well educated, affluent, and resentful of any kind of authority. Organizational development strategies predicated on yesterday's realities stand little chance of success in tomorrow's world.

In the 1970s American managers often blamed organized labor for our productivity problems. But high unemployment rates and the Reagan administration's antilabor policies rendered organized labor impotent in the 1980s. Among the more destructive results of increasingly egocentric and autocratic management policies are poor morale, disloyalty, declining productivity, and an inability to compete effectively in the international marketplace.

The rules of the game have changed both in the United States and in Russia. The old ways of coercing and intimidating employees don't work any longer. If the senior management of a company is serious about wanting to improve its productivity and competitive position abroad, it may have to pay the high price of sharing power with its employees.

As evidence of the undemocratic nature of American companies, union membership has declined from 30 percent in the 1970s to only 16 percent of the workforce—in contrast to 60 percent in Austria and 85 percent in Sweden. Furthermore, there is little evidence to suggest that our military-industrial complex is any more democratic or uses tactics that are any different from those of its Russian counterpart.

Graduate schools of business have done little to curb the alienation among blue-collar workers. If anything, they may actually have exacerbated the problem. Their attitude toward blue-collar workers is often arrogant and condescending. They have little interest in the problems of Johnny and Sasha.

Business schools do little to discourage the "anything goes" attitude, which prevails in the corporate executive suite. The new breed of "me first" managers trained in graduate schools of business is not uncomfortable with insider trading, hostile takeovers, bribery of foreign officials, and heavy-handed antiunion tactics.

Problems of meaninglessness in Russia are further compounded by the fact that for more than seventy years the Russian people lived in a society free of economic risks. The absence of risk and the heretofore limited possibilities for significant improvements in the quality of their lives have taken their toll on the Russians.

Until very recently, neither Russian enterprise managers nor employees had much decision-making power. All important decisions were made in Moscow. Central planners decided what should be produced, how it should be produced, how it should be distributed, and what price should be charged. Decisions on wages, employment, training, safety, and local working conditions were also made in Moscow. In a way similar to that of their counterparts in the United States, Russian workers were not encouraged to participate in important decisions affecting the enterprise where they worked and thus their individual lives. Is it any wonder that Johnny and Sasha are alienated?

The story of Johnny and Sasha is a story about separation. Although life may indeed be meaningful, meaning often eludes those who find themselves unable to connect with either their own inner self, other people, or some source of grounding. When this is the case, the inability to overcome one's separation becomes a spiritual, an intellectual, and an emotional obstacle to one's search for meaning.

*W*ho has not, at some time, been lonely in the midst of a social event? The feeling of our separation from the rest of life is most acute when we are surrounded by it in noise and talk. We realize then much more than in moments of solitude how strange we are to each other, how estranged life is from life. Each one of us draws back into himself. We cannot penetrate the hidden centre of another individual; nor can that individual pass beyond the shroud that covers our own being.

PAUL TILLICH
The Shaking of the Foundations [2]

People whose lives are detached and disconnected are prone to suffer from a number of anxieties:

1. The tension created by the conflict between personal freedom and human destiny
2. Isolation and emptiness
3. The fear of death

Freedom

Personal freedom, according to psychologist Rollo May, involves the possibility of self-actualization through individual initiative, personal choice, and spontaneous interaction. It entails "being able to harbor different possibilities in one's mind even though it is not clear at the moment which way one must act."[3] Dr. May goes on to contrast freedom with slavery, which he equates with powerlessness. "Freedom is the capacity to pause in the face of stimuli from many directions at once and . . . to throw one's weight toward this response rather than that one."[4]

Our physical characteristics, our intelligence, and our family background are among the givens in our lives. They constitute our *destiny*. If there is a God, God too is presumably a part of our destiny. The problem of life is how to use our personal *freedom* to confront our destiny so that we avoid being jerked around by our external environment—our family, our friends, our work, our government, and society as a whole. How can we take control of our lives without being driven by someone else or events such as the weather, natural disasters, the economy, or global politics? The tension between our freedom and destiny may either be a source of boundless energy and exhilaration or lead to debilitating anxiety and depression. According to Irvin D. Yalom, "He who does not obey himself is ruled by others. It is easier, far easier, to obey another than to command oneself."[5]

In his classic work *Escape from Freedom*,[6] Erich Fromm suggested two options for overcoming the unbearable powerlessness and loneliness associated with separation. On the one hand, we can use our freedom spontaneously to enhance our ability to create, to love, and to endure pain and suffering. By simply being ourselves we can reap the benefits of the quest for meaning—intellectual growth, emotional integrity, and physiological balance. On the other hand, we can give up our freedom, either by surrendering our individuality and integrity to some outside authority, such as our boss, a religious leader, or a military dictator like Hitler, Stalin, or Mao, or by engaging in destructive behavior or becoming a knee-jerk conformist.

The problem of most people living in affluent Western industrial democracies is that we have too much freedom rather than too little. We suffer from what Alvin Toffler in *Future Shock* called "the peril of over choice." We have an overwhelming number of choices with regard to religious beliefs, political ideology, employment possibilities, and consumer goods and services. Opportunities for how we spend our time and money are limitless. The question asked most often by college students these days is, How should I go about deciding what I want to be when I grow up? Unfortunately, colleges and universities do very little to help their students come to terms with this tough question.

Without a well-developed sense of meaning, the way in which we exercise our boundless freedom will be strongly influenced by our personal whims, the wishes of others, the marketplace, fads, and domestic and international political events.

In his best-seller *The Road Less Traveled,* M. Scott Peck notes that life is made difficult by the process of confronting our destiny and attempting to solve life's problems by exercising our freedom. It is through the discipline of confronting and solving problems that life becomes meaningful. Peck describes four tools of discipline:

1. Delaying gratification
2. Acceptance of responsibility
3. Dedication to truth
4. Balancing

Peck admonishes us to take our losses first and confront the associated pain before experiencing the pleasure that may accrue at some later time. Even in a society steeped in hedonism and the philosophy of instant gratification, this book has sold more than seven million copies!

Responsibility is the very essence of human existence. According to Peck we cannot solve life's problems unless we assume responsibility for their solution. He differentiates between *neurotics,* who assume they are responsible for all the world's problems, and those who suffer from *character disorders,* who blame all their problems on someone else. One of life's most stressful problems is deciding what we are and what we are not responsible for in this world.

Peck views truth and reality as forms of mapmaking. "If the map is true and accurate, we will generally know where we are, and if we have decided where we want to go, we will generally know how to get there. If the map is false and inaccurate, we will generally be lost."[7] If our maps of life are to be useful, they must continually be revised and they must not withhold pertinent information about reality.

By *balancing* Peck means that in order to solve life's problems we usually have to give up something. Life is full of trade-offs. Rarely do we get something for nothing. The bottom-line message of balancing is, "You can't have it all."

Theologian Reinhold Niebuhr accurately portrayed the tension that exists between freedom and destiny in his famous prayer:

God, give us grace to accept with serenity the things that cannot be changed, courage to change the things that should be changed, and the wisdom to distinguish the one from the other.[8]

Isolation

Although it may be possible to find meaning in life, meaning often eludes those who are separated from themselves, from others, and from the center of their being.

Nothing better illustrates the conflict between the very human need for attachment to other humans on the one hand, and the need for separation and independence on the other, than Alexander Naylor's behavior when he was two years old. While vigorously asserting his newfound independence, the most poignant words he uttered were, "My mommy, be with me" and "My dadda, be close to me."

> *A*ll the lonely people, where do they all belong?
>
> JOHN LENNON AND PAUL MCCARTNEY
> *"Eleanor Rigby"*

We are exhorted by radio, television, newspaper, politicians, educators, business leaders, and the clergy that to be a good American is to be a rugged individual. We are repeatedly encouraged to "do your own thing." "Freedom of Choice Makes America Great," so say the Chevrolet advertisements. Yet in our family life, work, play, religion, and politics, most Americans behave as mindless conformists. Freedom is uninteresting if buying a Chevrolet is the most significant thing we can do with it. While recognizing that our very existence depends on our uniqueness and separateness, most people fear the loneliness and existential emptiness of being isolated from other people. Whether or not we achieve a sense of meaning depends on how we confront our conflicting needs for separation and togetherness.

Hear that lonesome whippoorwill?
He sounds too blue to fly.
The midnight train is whining low,
I'm so lonesome I could cry.

HANK WILLIAMS
"I'm So Lonesome I Could Cry"

The notion of separation underlies Karl Marx's definition of alienation and Paul Tillich's definition of sin—separation from oneself, from others, and from one's grounding. Clearly our deserted island inhabitant is separated from others. Does our separation imply that we also will be alienated from the ground of our being—which Tillich calls God? Is it possible to tolerate the isolation and loneliness of the island, or would the separation from one's friends and loved ones drive one to despair and eventually suicide? As Tillich said, "We are only in a world through a community of men. And we can discover our souls only through the mirror of those who look at us. There is no depth of life without the depth of the common life."[9]

Few philosophers have had a better grasp of the very human problems of alienation and meaninglessness than did Karl Marx. Yet no philosopher has been more misunderstood in the West—particularly in the United States. Marx is perceived by most Americans as a godless atheist steeped in materialism and opposed to individualism and spiritual values of any sort. Nothing could be farther from the truth.

There are several reasons why this distorted view of Marx has persisted so long after his death in 1883. First and foremost was Soviet dictator Joseph V. Stalin's fraudulent use of Marx's name to justify the tyrannical form of communism he imposed on the Soviet people. In reality Soviet communism was the antithesis of what Marx had in mind. Second, out of ignorance most Americans chose to accept at face value Stalin's misrepresentations of Marx. It did not matter whether one had ever read Marx—which few had done. Everyone felt free to express opinions about him. Third, since private property lies at the core of American political ideology,

Marx's strident criticisms of its dehumanizing consequences enraged American business and political leaders. Fourth, Marx represented a serious threat to organized religion because he criticized the restrictions imposed on the human mind by some forms of faith. Marx saw how religion is often used by the powerful to keep people powerless.

Now that Stalinist communism has been thoroughly discredited both in the Soviet Union and Eastern Europe, maybe it is possible to step back and examine more objectively and less emotionally the Marxist analysis of alienation and emancipation. Specifically, what, if anything, did Marx have to say about the search for meaning?

Alienation

$\mathcal{M}$odern man has transformed himself into a commodity; he experiences his life energy as an investment with which he should make the highest profit, considering his position and the situation on the personality market. He is alienated from himself, from his fellow men, and from nature. His main aim is profitable exchange of his skills, knowledge, and of himself, his "personality package" with others who are equally intent on a fair and profitable exchange. Life has no goal except the one to move, no principle except the one of fair exchange, no satisfaction except the one to consume.

ERICH FROMM
The Art of Loving[10]

To Marx life was not inherently meaningless, but rather became meaningless as a result of the alienation people experienced in dehumanized nineteenth-century capitalist society. Marx's philosophy was a protest against this alienation and what he perceived as the transformation of people—particularly working-class people—into things. If anything, Marx actually understated the problems of alienation we face in Western industrial nations today. He did not foresee the day when alienation would become the fate of the vast majority—not just blue-collar workers. Among the other social groups in America who appear to be especially alienated are: migrant workers, some women, artists, substance abusers, juvenile delinquents, some ethnic minorities, and the racially prejudiced; in short, people who feel cut off from the means of power.

Consider the forty-five-year-old accountant who has been director of accounting for a large defense contractor for the past five years. His job is extremely boring, and he is only rarely consulted by senior management on matters of strategic importance. One day while driving to work, he realizes not only is his secret ambition to become the company president a fantasy, but that he will never move any higher up the corporate ladder. The sheer horror of remaining in the same boring job for another twenty years precipitates a severe anxiety attack followed by months of debilitating depression.

Hardly a month goes by in which there is not at least one article in the business press about some well-known corporate executive who has opted out of corporate life to pursue a quieter, more reflective existence far removed from the executive suite. Often referred to as a "mid-life identity crisis," this phenomenon may also be caused by the absence of a sense of purpose or meaning in the lives of these high-level executives. In all too many firms, senior executives are forced to subscribe to the values of the company in order to advance up the corporate ladder. The values they must embrace place too much emphasis on greed, the acquisition of power, and the desire to dominate and manipulate others. For such executives, motivation comes not from internal, personal goals but from recognition and approval by others. Eventually, this type of behavior results in anxiety, depression, feelings of emptiness, and burnout. Some executives turn to drugs and alcohol to combat their loneliness and emptiness. Indeed, it is not surprising that there are hundreds of stress-management programs in the United States today.

More than ten million Americans are affected by a pathological response to isolation and loneliness known as borderline personality disorder (BPD).[11] Some of the symptoms of this disorder include unstable relationships, self-destructiveness, severe mood swings, fits of rage, suicidal threats, low self-esteem, fear of abandonment, and chronic feelings of boredom and emptiness. Although many people suffer from one or more of these symptoms, what differentiates borderline personalities from others is the intensity with which they experience these symptoms. Although BPD is one of the most common psychiatric disorders, it is also one of the most frustrating to treat. Some psychotherapists avoid borderline personalities like the plague. Perhaps these patients serve as an all-too-vivid reminder of the therapist's own state of separation and meaninglessness. Anorexia and bulimia, two well-known eating disorders, also can be triggered by separation.

Another effect of isolation and loneliness is *somatization*—bodily complaints for which there is no evidence of any physiological illness. The conversion of anxiety and stress into bodily symptoms often gives rise to *hypochondria* as well.

Effects of Separation

Spiritual   ──────▶ Detachment
Intellectual   ──────▶ Alienation
Emotional   ──────▶ Anxiety
Physiological ──────▶ Somatization

That millions of American adults are alienated should come as no surprise, when one examines the plight of American youth—children, teenagers, and college students. Sylvia Hewlett writes in her book *When the Bough Breaks,* that compared with youth in other affluent nations children in America are "more likely to die before their first birthday; to live in poverty; to be abandoned by their fathers; and to be killed before the age of twenty-five."[12] Even though the United States is one of the wealthiest countries in the world, we do "not even make it into the top ten on any significant indicator of child welfare."

We have one of the highest infant mortality rates in the industrialized West. Among rich nations we are number one in the percentage of children living below the poverty line (22 percent), number one in the incidence of teenage pregnancies (one million a year), and number one in the homicide rate for males between fifteen and twenty-four years old. In 1989, at least 900,000 children were physically or sexually abused. The number of children in foster care exceeds 340,000, and the number of homeless children is estimated to be well over 200,000. Twelve million children are uninsured and have little or no access to health care.

As we noted earlier, from what we have observed on college campuses, there is little evidence to suggest that the plight of American teenagers improves once they enter college. If anything, their problems become even worse.

On the night Duke University won the national basketball championship for the second consecutive year, several inebriated students sustained severe burns while attempting to jump over a huge bonfire. Several others were injured by shards of glass from flying bottles. A dormitory brawl involving a dozen students, some of whom were armed with knives and guns, resulted in one student's being knocked unconscious. A few hours later two Russian businessmen attending an executive education program at Duke's Fuqua Business School were killed when their car traveling 85 mph crashed into a tree half a mile from the Fuqua School where they had been celebrating.

At Duke and many other places, free beer-keg parties provide the energy and focus for most campus social life. For students, keg parties represent an illusory attempt to deal with their separation and meaninglessness. Many students experience a kind of love-hate relationship with keg parties. On the one hand, they can't seem to live without them. On the other hand, many women report feelings of alienation, depression, and despair on the morning after. Kegs have resulted in a steady stream of alcohol-related emergency room visits by Duke students, reports of alcohol counseling, and extensive damage to residence halls. Nationwide, alcohol is a factor in the majority of the rapes among college-age students. Feminists describe acquaintance rape as a male-female power problem. We see it as a symptom of alienation and meaninglessness among youth. Such behavior is constantly reinforced by incessant beer and wine advertising during televised collegiate sporting events, aimed at college students—many of whom are under the legal drinking age.

Message to Michael

When eleven-year-old Michael was admitted to the hospital after overdosing on his mother's antidepressants, he was wearing an expensive black leather jacket and leather pants. The response of his father with whom he was living was, "How could you do this to me? For Christmas I gave you ten of the eleven things on your wish list." The list included a VCR, a personal computer, and a telephone answering machine for his private telephone line.

When asked about his suicide attempt, Michael said that he felt isolated, lonely, and unloved by his father even though they spent each evening together. According to Michael, his father would arrive at their downtown apartment each evening around 5:30 P.M., fix himself a drink and read the *New York Times*. It was understood that his father was not to be interrupted during this sacred time. At 6:00 P.M. they would watch the local news together followed by the national news.

Then his father would prepare dinner alone, since he did not like to have anyone else in the kitchen while he was cooking. Michael would start doing his homework. When Michael's dinner was ready—usually consisting of hamburgers—he would then eat by himself while his father had another couple of drinks. After Michael finished eating, his father would fix himself a steak or something else which he liked, and Michael would go to his room. Very often the father would fall asleep on the couch. Michael usually stayed up until after midnight playing video games and listening to rock music. Even though Michael was very intelligent, getting him off to school each morning was a major ordeal.

The father denied that he was an alcoholic and refused additional treatment for himself and Michael after Michael was released from the hospital.

But what about the "forgotten" 50 percent of high school students who don't go to college? A U.S. Labor Department report prepared by a blue-ribbon commission expressed surprise and dismay that those students who leave high school and don't go to college are ill prepared to enter the workforce. The study found that these students lacked the ability to solve problems, make decisions, accept responsibility, work on teams, and manage their own time. The commission placed most of the blame for these problems on our public schools. No attention was devoted to the possible effects on high school students of being reared by parents whose lives are meaningless.

We expect our public schools to solve all our social, economic, and political problems, and then are disappointed when they don't meet our expectations. Children who grow up in impoverished, broken homes where there is no sense of meaning have their work cut out for them, even if they are bused to shiny, new upscale schools in the more affluent suburbs. Unfortunately, neither our underfinanced public schools nor our well-heeled private schools seem to be able to do much about the problems of alienation and meaninglessness.

Another group of particularly alienated people in the United States is the elderly. That infirm older people living in nursing homes are often depressed should come as no surprise to anyone. What is surprising though is the extent of alienation one finds in upscale retirement complexes, which offer independent living with special services to residents who are still able to take care of themselves.

Hundreds of such institutions sprang up all over the country during the 1980s in response to increased affluence as well as an unwillingness on the part of some families to have aging parents remain with them in the home. Some people reside in these complexes by choice. Those who have been sent there against their will are often angry and depressed.

Although the physical condition of these retirement homes is usually excellent, the competence of management in dealing with the elderly often leaves much to be desired. As a result of inexperienced management, there is frequently no sense of community among residents, who bicker endlessly over the food service and fight over who sits at which dining room table. When someone dies or is taken to the hospital, no one really seems to care. There is no concern for, "How can we collectively make the best of our remaining years together? What can we do to help each other prepare to die?" Death is rarely mentioned. No effort is made to come to terms with its inevitability. Many are angry, depressed, noncooperative, and egocentric. If one has not found meaning before entering one of these depressing places, it is not likely to be found there. Is it any wonder that many of the elderly have become addicted to drug-induced sleep?

The Pain of Old Age

The real pain of old age . . . the horror of living an unobserved life.

IRVIN D. YALOM
When Nietzsche Wept[13]

Drug abuse and violent crime are among the most destructive ways in which Americans deal with alienation and meaninglessness. Although we don't imprison people for their political beliefs or block them from leaving the country, we are nevertheless one of the most violent nations in the world. We have the highest homicide rate and we are first in the percentage of the population incarcerated—ahead of South Africa and the former Soviet Union. Homicide is the sixth leading cause of premature death in the United States, occurring at a rate 4.4 times higher than in the next most violent Western industrial nation.

From a very early age Americans are bombarded with television violence beginning with the Saturday morning cartoons. The average sixteen-year-old has seen more than 100,000 acts of violence on TV. Children who witnessed the 1991 edition of the Ringling Brothers and Barnum & Bailey Circus were treated to a particularly heavy dose of violence including the Double-Barreled Human Canon, the Wheel of Death, the Globe of Death motorcycle act, and David Larible—the knife throwing clown. The Eliminator TS-7, a toy weapon sold by F.A.O. Schwarz for ages five and up, was advertised as "the ultimate sound-and-light defense system." This awesome 7-in-1 weapon includes a power dagger, a power sword, a laser sword, an army machine gun, a cyber gun, and a super eliminator. Recently, trading cards that depict well-known killers and gangsters instead of sports stars have begun appearing in the marketplace. Among the criminals whose pictures appear on such cards are California's Zodiac killer, New York's "Son of Sam," Ted Bundy, and Milwaukee's Jeffrey Dahmer, who was convicted of killing, dismembering, and in some cases eating sixteen young men. Not surprisingly, on an average day, 135,000 children bring guns to school.

Shortly after American troops were sent to Somalia in 1992, a graphic cartoon depicting handgun violence in America appeared in the *Cincinnati Enquirer*. The cartoon posed the following question: "Where is the U.S. working the hardest to curb the use of guns?" Answer: "Somalia."

Many colleges and universities still offer credit for courses in R.O.T.C. But the aim of R.O.T.C. is to train young Americans to be efficient killers. Paradoxically, while American medical schools are teaching physicians how to save lives, professors of military science at these same institutions are helping produce more trained killers. When the University of Richmond needed a keynote speaker for the dedication of its new Jepson Leadership School, it turned to General H. Norman "Stormin' Norman" Schwarzkopf, the man who orchestrated the computer-controlled, high-tech deaths of 200,000 Iraqis during the Persian Gulf War.

Is it any wonder that President John F. Kennedy, Senator Robert F. Kennedy, and Dr. Martin Luther King, Jr., were gunned down at the hands of assassins, or that Presidents Gerald Ford and Ronald Reagan as well as Governor George Wallace were also the targets of assassination attempts? Hardly a week goes by in which we don't read about a multiple homicide somewhere in the United States.

Two weeks after Bill Clinton was elected President, the Secret Service forced the Central Florida Young Republicans Club to cancel its annual "turkey shoot" fundraiser. The Young Republicans had planned to use enlarged photos of President-elect Clinton as bull's-eye targets.

To combat violent crime and drug abuse, we call for tougher law enforcement, capital punishment, and more prisons—none of which seem to work. No matter how tempting it may be to bomb the drug lords of Colombia and Peru, there is no military solution to America's drug problem. People take drugs because they are alienated and powerless and have no sense of meaning in their lives. All the aircraft carriers and battleships in the world will not make Americans less dependent on drugs. Drug abuse and violence are very human problems and cry out for human solutions, not public relations gimmicks or government enforcement programs.

No matter which label we use—alcoholic, drug addict, child abuser, rapist, murderer, or polluter—all are examples of the consequences of separation and alienation for which our political leaders have little understanding or empathy. Our nation lacks direction. Having lost our Soviet enemy, there is no vision of the future beyond the cold war.

Denial of Death

The aura of death was everywhere as Dominika walked through the tall grass in the Brodnowski Cemetery in Warsaw, Poland, searching for the grave of her father. One of the largest cemeteries in all of Europe, Brodnowski was particularly busy that day as one funeral procession after another wound its way through the eerie maze of unkempt graves. Even though Dominika's father had died nine months earlier, her mother had withheld the news of his death fearing "it might upset Dominika."

Our fear of death—the ultimate form of separation—is the third form of existential anxiety we shall consider. It stems from our dread of the complete loss of control over our lives and the possibility that death may lead to nothingness. To cope with our fear of death, we spend our entire lives denying that we are going to die. No writer was ever more preoccupied with death than Edgar Allan Poe.

Annabel Lee

*F*or the moon never beams, without bringing me dreams
   Of the beautiful ANNABEL LEE,
And the stars never rise, but I feel the bright eyes
   Of the beautiful ANNABEL LEE:
And so, all the night-tide, I lie down by the side
Of my darling—my darling—my life and my bride,
   In the sepulchre there by the sea—
   In her tomb by the sounding sea.

                              EDGAR ALLAN POE

In his powerful book *The Denial of Death,* Ernest Becker describes two different neurotic responses to the fear of dying—self-love and withdrawal.[14] For some people the fear of ceasing to be and losing oneself leads to an escape path based on the pursuit of competence, material wealth, power, and control. This form of self-love is often displayed in the actions of athletic superstars, political dema-gogues, business tycoons, movie stars, famous rock musicians, and television evangelists. Rather than confront the pain caused by their fear of nothingness, these compulsive individuals resort to heroism, imperishable monuments, work addiction, manipulation, and control as a means of denying their mortality. By staying busy, they hope to push aside forever their intense fear of death. "They create ever-more-intricate societies to soften the blow of death by simulating a physical and social eternity on earth."[15]

On the other hand, there are those who are so afraid of dying that they simply freeze whenever they contemplate the possibility of their own demise. To overcome their self-imposed paralysis, such people seek the protection of an omnipotent intercessor such as a personal god or on a more ephemeral level—a priest, a rabbi, a physician, a psychologist, or a mentor. But with those who suffer from this second type of neurosis, there is always a serious problem of lack of trust of the rescuer. There is always a tendency to withdraw from life and avoid committing to anyone or any set of values and beliefs. Because they are so afraid of dying, they can never enjoy life.

Thus one type of neurotic merges with the surrounding environment, becomes too much a part of it, and loses his or her claim on life. The other type severs ties with the outside world and eventually loses the ability to function in the world on its terms. Some people find it very difficult to separate, others find it equally difficult to unite. The challenge is to strike a balance between separation and merger.

Eva Peron

*Y*ou were supposed to have been immortal. . . . But in the end, you could not deliver.

Evita

Two forms of death denial which enjoy widespread public acceptance in the United States are high-tech medicine and sophisticated military weapons systems such as SDI.

For those who can afford health insurance, the sky is the limit when it comes to the use of magnetic resonance imaging, ultrasound, nuclear diagnostics, complex multi-organ transplants, coronary bypass surgery, artificial kidney machines, death-defying prenatal procedures, and emergency helicopter service. Our favorite high-tech medical procedure is the pig liver transplant, which enables the swine's organ to live on long after the death of its original owner.

Intensive-care medicine is by far the most expensive form of medical care money can buy. We have more than 87,000 intensive-care beds in the United States—more than any other country in the world. America devotes more than 12 percent of its GNP to its high-tech medicine—more than any other industrialized nation. More than 80 percent of our lifetime expenditure for health care occurs in the last six months of our lives, in which "health care" is a euphemism for six months of futile death care.

Ironically, America's huge investment in death denial through medical high-technology has had little effect on life expectancy or the incidence of sickness by comparison with other developed countries. Overall, Americans die younger, lose more babies, and are at least as apt to suffer from chronic disease as those living in other industrial nations that spend much less on medical care.

Just as the Egyptian pharaohs had their pyramids and the Turkish sultans had their mosques, so too did President Ronald Reagan have his Strategic Defense Initiative, popularly known as Star Wars. That Reagan was so attracted to SDI should have come as no surprise given his penchant for large-scale, high-tech enterprises such as the B-1 bomber, the MX missile, the Stealth bomber, the Trident II submarine, the Clinch River Breeder Reactor, the Space Shuttle, the Space Station, and the Super Collider. Reagan and his Secretary of Defense Caspar Weinberger never encountered a high-tech weapons system they did not wish to buy—and the more expensive the better.

Inspired by anti-Soviet physicist Edward Teller and the 1940s film *Murder in the Air,* on March 23, 1983, President Reagan called on scientists to develop the Strategic Defense Initiative—a missile defense shield in space that would render nuclear weapons "impotent and obsolete."

As originally envisaged, SDI would consist of a complex network of systems including X-ray laser beams; particle beams; electromagnetic "sling-shots," which would hurl nonexplosive projectiles called "brilliant pebbles" through space at great speed; and sensing, tracking, and aiming devices. All these systems require the extraordinary coordination of advanced computers and other technologies to detect missiles, compute their trajectories, and direct intercepting weapons over great distances.

In his 1986 State of the Union address, President Reagan was almost euphoric over SDI:

> Technology transforming our lives can solve the greatest problem of the twentieth century. A security shield can one day render nuclear weapons obsolete and free mankind from the prison of nuclear terror.

It was our neurotic fear of death that drove us to spend nearly $11 trillion on the cold war and ultimately to seek refuge under the nuclear umbrella of Star Wars—the most imaginative death-denying technology of all time. Even though the cold war is over and the Soviet Union has been completely dismantled, we continue to spend several billion dollars annually on anti-missile systems.

No longer able to use the Soviet Union as a credible threat on which to justify their sophisticated space weapons, compulsive weapons scientists have turned to the threat of cosmic bombardment to rationalize the latest missiles and nuclear warheads. Their attention has been captured by a comet called "Swift-Tuttle," which is said to have a one-in-ten-thousand chance of hitting the earth sometime in the next century. Trading heavily on the fear of such an event, these scientists propose to spend billions of dollars tracking and eventually diverting Swift-Tuttle away from the earth. Their doomsday forecasts have an all-too-familiar ring to them.

After reading the passages on death in Ecclesiastes to our undergraduate students at Duke each semester, we ask them what comes to mind when they contemplate their own death. Their responses usually include separation, powerlessness, loss of control, meaninglessness, and nothingness. Magdalena once replicated this exercise with first-year medical students at the Medical College of Virginia. Their overall response was, "We don't think about dying. Death is for the very old, not the young." The undergraduates openly acknowledged their fear of death. The medical students, who were preparing to spend their entire careers confronting death, were engaged in utter denial of an integral part of their work.

From the company that brought us Charles Manson and Jeffrey Dahmer serial-killer trading cards comes a macabre form of death denial—trading cards featuring people who either have AIDS or have died of AIDS. Among the celebrities included in the new AIDS series are Rock Hudson, Arthur Ashe, and Magic Johnson. Purchasers receive a free condom with each set of cards.

Although many of us spend our lives denying that we are going to die, some like Albert Camus have discovered that death is an important source of meaning. The fact that life is finite makes every remaining moment precious and beautiful. In a very real sense, life without death would not be worthwhile. Death liberates us from the present and grants us the wisdom to sort out our priorities as to how best to use our remaining time on earth. By earnestly contemplating our own death, we may begin to learn how to live in such a way that we avoid the pitfalls of a life based entirely on either self-love or withdrawal.

Our Common Plight

The picture we have painted of separation is not much prettier than our portrayal of meaninglessness. Spiritual detachment, intellectual alienation, emotional anxiety, and somatization provide little more appeal than despair, nihilism, depression, and death. Separation, meaninglessness, and death are facts of the human condition. But how shall we respond to our common destiny—through acceptance, denial, or confrontation?

This and the foregoing chapter have examined the bleak consequences of separation and meaninglessness. In the next chapter we consider the effects of the denial of the human condition through consumerism, the accumulation of wealth, religious orthodoxy, legalism, and political ideology. For those who wish to confront the human condition rather than either accept it or deny it, there is a third option—being. Beginning with chapter 5 and continuing through chapter 10, we discuss how one can take responsibility for one's own meaning through being rather than having. Specifically, we show how separation, meaninglessness, and death can become positive forces in our search for meaning, thus reducing our chances of dying unhappy.

Chapter 4

HAVING

A society whose principles are acquisition, profit, and property produces a social character oriented around having, and once the dominant pattern is established, nobody wants to be an outsider, or indeed an outcast; in order to avoid this risk everybody adapts to the majority, who have in common only their mutual antagonism.

ERICH FROMM
TO HAVE OR TO BE

Shortly before he died of a brain tumor in 1991, Republican presidential campaign advisor Lee Atwater—architect of George Bush's highly effective 1988 Willie Horton campaign advertisements—lamented, "The '80s were about acquiring—acquiring wealth, power, prestige. I know. I acquired more wealth, power and prestige than most. But you can acquire all you want and still feel empty."[1] Atwater took note of the "spiritual vacuum at the heart of American society," which he called the "tumor of our soul."

To escape the separation, loneliness, boredom, depression, and despair associated with meaninglessness, the living dead seek meaning by embracing a life-style based almost entirely on having. Through the accumulation of material goods and wealth, adventurism, environmental gluttony, political power, religious orthodoxy, health fetishism, and even violence, they hope to numb the effects of the pain and suffering which accompany their separation and meaninglessness. Owning, possessing, manipulating, and controlling are all parts of the modus operandi of life in the having mode. In response to their insatiable psychological and sensory needs, those who are into having often exhibit behavioral patterns which are aggressive, competitive, and antagonistic. To have someone or something is to take charge of it or to conquer it. Robbing, killing, overpowering, and consuming are all forms of having. Those in the having mode are afraid of losing what they have either to someone else or to the government or possibly through death.

To reduce the risk of losing what they have, they save and hoard money and material things endlessly.

We are a nation obsessed with having and consuming people and things. We are so preoccupied with having that we have lost our ability to be human beings. Our happiness depends mostly on our superiority to others, on our power, and on our ability to manipulate others. Capitalist America may be the most efficient and productive nation in the world, but it extracts a high human cost. Conspicuous consumption is no longer a sign of our success, but rather of our spiritual vacuum.

Hedonism

Recent surveys indicate that 90 percent of all Americans identify with some organized religion. Nearly 60 percent of the population are members of a church, synagogue, or other religious congregation. Ironically, the only two religions to which many Americans are truly committed—individualism and hedonism—were not included in either of these surveys. Although we like to think of ourselves as a Judeo-Christian nation, we are in fact a nation of super individualists and hedonists masked as Baptists, Catholics, Methodists, and Jews.

In the words of television producer Norman Lear,

> Our popular culture celebrates the material and largely ignores the spiritual. Greed is the order of the day in a society preoccupied at all levels with the pursuit of bottom lines, a society which celebrates consumption, careerism and winning. . . . We have become a numbers-oriented culture that puts more faith in what we can see, touch, and hear, and is suspicious of the unquantifiable, the intuitive, and the mysterious.[2]

What life is all about for most Americans is "looking out for number one." President Ronald Reagan once told the American people that "what I want to see above all is that this country remains a country where someone can always get rich." This is one promise that he most assuredly kept.

Capitalist Blowout

*B*etween 1977 and 1989, three-fourths of the gain in pre-tax, real income of all American families went to the wealthiest 660,000 families. The average pretax income of families in the highest bracket increased by 77 percent from $315,000 to $560,000 in constant dollars. During this same period, the typical American family—a median income family—saw its income increase by only 4 percent to $36,000. Those in the bottom 40 percent of families actually experienced a decline in constant dollar income.[3]

Those who were the most successful in taking care of themselves during the 1980s were the very rich. Not only did the rich get richer in the 1980s, but they also became stingier. They gave a far smaller share of their income to charity than was previously the case. In 1979, people who earned incomes of more than $1 million (in 1991 dollars) gave more than 7 percent of their after-tax income to charity. Twelve years later that figure had dropped to less than 4 percent.[4] While the wealthy were reaping the benefits of Ronald Reagan's free market blowout in the 1980s, the number of workers earning wages below the poverty level nearly doubled. In 1979 there were 7.8 million workers with incomes below the poverty line. By 1990 that number had risen to 14.4 million.

Nothing better illustrates the extent to which greed has been embraced in America than the compensation of senior executives of large companies. While real wages were declining and corporate profits were flat in the 1980s, the salaries of corporate executives were soaring. During the past two decades, the pay of an average worker expressed in constant dollars and adjusted for taxes decreased by 13 percent, while the adjusted pay of the average CEO of a large American company rose more than four times. American CEOs earn 160 times more than an average worker, while their Japanese and German counterparts earn 16 and 21 times more, respectively.[5] Junk-bond king Michael R. Milken established a new high-water mark in corporate pay when he received $550 million from Drexel Burnham Lambert in a single year. When Sam Walton, founder of Wal-Mart, died in 1992, he was thought to be the wealthiest person in America. The shares of Wal-Mart stock held collectively by his family were valued at $23 billion at the time of his death.

Since its inception our nation has taken pride in being a global melting pot of immigrants. As evidence of how far our obsession with money and power has evolved, the U.S. Immigration and Naturalization Service introduced a new "millionaire visa" in 1991 aimed at attracting foreign investors to the United States. To foreigners who invest $1 million or more in a business that employs at least ten persons, our government is prepared to issue "special visas," which include permanent residency status—the first step toward citizenship. In other words, to become a United States citizen it no longer matters who you are, but rather how much you have.

Addiction to marijuana, cocaine, heroin, or other habit-forming drugs can lead to arrest, conviction, and imprisonment in the United States. But addiction to beer, cigarettes, junk foods, television, video games, automobiles, personal computers, designer clothes, shopping malls, credit cards, high-tech toys, and plastic yuck is not only considered acceptable behavior, but is strongly encouraged by every conceivable form of advertising. So powerful is the drive to consume in America, that consumer sovereignty and consumer freedom-of-choice dominate all other human rights— civil, political, and economic. To be a good American is to be a big consumer. Who you are depends on what you have and what you consume.

Reinforced by parents, preschool teachers, television, and peers, addiction to material goods begins at a very early age. Even though three-year-old Alexander Naylor was admonished to avoid a life based on having, one trip to Toys "R" Us, which boasts more than a million toys in stock, would undo several months of effort by his parents to dissuade him from his materialistic ways. Every time he set foot in one of these seductive toy boutiques he went completely amuck—running frantically up and down the aisles demanding one of everything. Is it possible that unbridled materialism is the American equivalent of the Great Satan?

Jewel-laden Choo Choo

A fully operative, solid-gold miniature train carrying rubies, diamonds, sapphires, and emeralds on a 41-foot track. Price: $100,000.

1992 Neiman Marcus Christmas Book

We have laws in this country against the seduction and molestation of children. Yet what child manipulators like Toys "R" Us and Showbiz Pizza do to the psyches of American children is unconscionable. How many children have been drawn to McDonald's restaurants by the irresistible attraction of a free plastic toy rather than a hamburger and french fries? Society pays dearly for the exploitative methods used by these merchants of hedonism to allay the boredom of the children of the living dead. Sunday school classes and bar mitzvah classes cannot undo the damage done by these juvenile pleasure palaces. Parents whose lives are meaningless and empty know no other options for their children than what others do—consume, consume, consume.

Zap Chicken Now Available

*P*oultry processors are now allowed to begin zapping chickens, turkeys, and game hens with gamma rays to kill bacteria.

New regulations permit federally approved poultry processing plants to use irradiation to treat fresh or frozen poultry. Poultry is passed through a chamber containing rods of radioactive cobalt-60 or cesium-137 where it is bombarded with gamma rays. Zapping destroys illness-causing bacteria, insects, and mold but does not reduce the effects of steroids and other growth enhancing drugs given to poultry by processors.

U.S. Department of Agriculture

The typical American family wants a large, expensive home with a big yard, dozens of high-tech electrical appliances, two or three automobiles, and enough plastic to pave over the entire neighborhood. On the other hand, affluent Western Europeans are likely to be content on average with more modest homes and fewer automobiles and electronic gadgets. People who live in cities such as Helsinki, Stockholm, and Vienna consume fewer resources per person because they live closer together, shop in their own neighborhood, and enjoy a greater sense of community than one finds in most American cities.

Shoppers in America have an overwhelming number of choices available to them. There are more shopping malls than high schools in the United States—nearly 35,000. A typical supermarket may have more than 30,000 items on its shelves—up from 9,000 items in 1976. As many as 3,000 new health and beauty-care products have been introduced in the United States in a single year along with 1,300 new beverages. Most of the profits earned by American retailers each year are generated in December from Christmas consumer spending binges. Easter, Washington's Birthday, Memorial Day, and the Fourth of July also are used by retailers to hype consumer goods.

The Mall of America

In August 1992 the Mall of America opened near Minneapolis-St. Paul, Minnesota. It covers 78 acres, is four stories tall, and has four major department stores, up to four hundred specialty shops, a 14-screen movie theater, dozens of restaurants, several nightclubs, a split-level high-tech miniature golf course, and a 7-acre indoor amusement park. It expects to employ ten thousand people and generate 40 million visits annually.

Eastern Europeans have been easily seduced by Western consumerism. Even before the collapse of the Soviet Union, Soviet visitors to the United States were often seen boarding Aeroflot flights back to Moscow laden with stereos, VCRs, and personal computers. When Tadeusz and his family from Warsaw visited the United States for the first time in 1991, they spent hours each day basking in the artificial glitter of Richmond shopping malls. There was barely enough room in the car for all of their luggage for the trip to Dulles Airport to board their return flight to Poland.

Isn't it interesting that the current debate over abortion pits "Freedom of Choice" against "Rights to Life"? This makes abortion sound like a consumer issue. Life becomes a right to be had; abortion becomes another life-style choice.

---

*E*verybody I know drinks the right beer when they ain't sippin' the right soft drink; they're using the right deodorant and rinsin' with the right conditioner.

NORMAN LEAR[6]

Not only are Americans obsessed with consumer goods, but also with spectator sports—particularly football, basketball, baseball, golf, and tennis. Because of their high TV entertainment value, athletic superstars receive millions of dollars in professional contracts and salaries. National Basketball Association players who played on the so-called Dream Team at the 1992 Olympic games in Barcelona stayed in $900-a-night hotel rooms. Millions of American men and some women vicariously live out their fantasies of becoming sports heroes by spending hours each week watching sports on television. Even though only one in a thousand high school athletes ever becomes a professional, almost half of all African American males who play ball in school believe they will play professional sports. And if we can't have it all—as we are promised on TV—we can at least dream about having it all by watching our favorite sports stars on television.

In addition to being television celebrities for their athletic abilities, sports heroes are also highly publicized for their sexual exploits off the playing field. Even before he contracted AIDS, the promiscuous life-style of basketball legend Magic Johnson was no secret to anyone. Wilt Chamberlain even boasted in his book that he had slept with 20,000 women.

Spectator sports in the United States are the American equivalent of the Roman games. Sports heroes are treated like pagan Roman gladiators. They are strong, self-assertive, and narcissistic. We conveniently overlook the dirty mixture of money, greed, and publicity that surrounds both professional and intercollegiate sports. Not unlike the consumption of material goods, spectator sports also are about having—fame, fortune, power, and sex. The only difference is that the sports spectator must experience all these pleasures vicariously through the exploits of others.

But addiction to television sportscasts is by no means limited to adults. Many children are so hooked on televised football, basketball, and baseball games that they have little incentive to play any of these sports themselves. They would much rather play a computer game than participate in a soccer match or play tennis. Our homes have been transformed into a farmland of couch potatoes—people too lazy to venture onto the playing field of life.

For many who became very rich during the 1980s, the novelty of mundane consumerism has begun to wane, and boredom has started to set in. This is particularly true of the wealthy intelligentsia. For them the appeal of another automobile, a second or third home, or one more high-tech plastic gadget has become quite marginal. They are into a quite different form of having—adventurism. These sophisticated consumers have turned to flying, sky-diving, hang-gliding, bungee jumping, mountain-climbing, spelunking, and scuba-diving in search of adventure. What these forms of adventure have in common is that they are often very dangerous and quite expensive. Bungee jumpers pay up to $65 a pop to leap off a 110-foot platform with their fate tied to an elastic cord.

Hoboing—illegally riding the rails—has become particularly popular among adventure-seeking affluent West Coast males. Few of the members of the National Hobo Association are real hoboes. Many are wealthy, bored men in search of romantic adventure. Riding freight trains across the country and then telling tall tales about their ventures fulfill a heartfelt need of some of these pilgrims.

The Eris Society attracts a fascinating group of wealthy libertarians, self-proclaimed anarchists, iconoclasts, technocrats, hoboes, and hedonists each August to Aspen, Colorado, to exchange stories of pleasure and adventure. Many of the members publish their own newsletters and catalogs offering advice, merchandise, and other services related to such diverse topics as the stock market, life extension, survival, and libertarianism. At a recent meeting, Eris founder Douglas Casey gave a lecture entitled "Hey Kid, You Too Can Own Your Own Third World Country." Casey is the author of *The International Man: The Complete Guidebook to the World's Last Frontiers, for Freedom Seekers, Investors, Adventurers, Speculators, and Expatriates.*

The environmental consequences of our addiction to the consumption of material goods are staggering. They include air and water pollution, acid rain, ozone depletion, excessive deforestation, soil degradation, and the destruction of the habitats of millions of species. What the affluent industrial nations of the world are involved in is nothing less than the rape of the entire planet for the short-term personal gain of a relatively small percentage of the world's population. The sins of pride, greed, and gluttony are not only offenses against society but offenses against nature as well.

Meet Me at the Mall

*A*merica's thousands of shopping malls are the centerpieces of the most environmentally destructive way of life yet devised. In combination, the suburbs that surround them, the cars that stream into them, the packaged throwaways that stream out of them, and the fast-food outlets and convenience franchises that mimic them cause more harm to the biosphere than anything else except perhaps rapid population growth.

Washington Post [7]

Although the United States accounts for 4.7 percent of the world's population, it is responsible for 22.3 percent of the deadly carbon dioxide buildup in the atmosphere—the principal cause of the greenhouse effect and global warming. This is in sharp contrast to China, which contains 21.0 percent of the world's population but accounts for only 10.9 percent of the world's carbon dioxide emissions. These figures are hardly surprising when one considers the fact that the United States is number one in the emission of air pollutants, in per capita energy consumption, and in the percentage of commuter trips made by private automobile rather than public transport.

At the same time the adage "Reduce, recycle, and reuse" is practiced extensively in Japan and Western Europe, we are the world's largest producer of garbage. On average each American throws away nearly 1,500 pounds of trash each year including food scraps, newspapers, containers and packaging, and lawn waste. We also discard nearly 200 million razor blades annually as well as more than 3 million unwanted household appliances. As environmentalist Michael McCloskey has said, "We are not immortal, but our acts are." He adds,

> The question is not why we exist but whether we deserve to exist as supposedly rational beings if we act like conquerors rather than caring beings willing to share the planet with all those who are less powerful, and to act with restraint in respecting the needs of others and all life to come.[8]

And how do our political leaders respond to the greed, radical materialism, adventurism, and environmental gluttony of a nation drowning in a sea of hedonism? They give us exactly what we want to hear from them—the politics of narcissism and instant gratification. Knowing our very low tolerance for pain and self-criticism, they dish out congratulatory self-aggrandizement. And we love every word of it. President Ronald Reagan's grasp of the politics of narcissism was without equal.

Legalism

To rationalize and support their individualism and hedonism and further avoid some of the terror associated with meaninglessness, many people turn to legalism to protect what they have. They do so through private property laws, political ideology, patriotism, militarism, and religious fundamentalism. For people who are looking for definitive amswers to life's unanswered questions, it is far easier to embrace someone else's answers than to confront these troubling questions on their own. Laws, law enforcement officials, political ideology, the military, and legalistic religions are in the business of providing specific answers to life's tough questions. Legalism is a very powerful and very popular form of the denial of meaninglessness.

If you are into having, above all you want to secure that which you perceive to be your own. That's what laws protecting private property are all about. To maintain control over your property, you need to use power to protect it from those who would try to take it away from you. They too can never have enough. The desire to have property on the part of the propertyless can lead to violence to steal property from others. The primary role of law enforcement officials is to enforce private property laws.

Western Democracies

*T*he Western democracies tend to have a problem with meaning. They promise their citizens a society in which each citizen is free to create his or her own meaning— meaning which, for most of us, becomes little more than the freedom to consume at ever higher levels.

STANLEY HAUERWAS AND
WILLIAM H. WILLIMON[9]

But to encourage those who have no property to respect the property of others, we must have a political ideology which rationalizes that some have property while others have none. That's where free market capitalism fits into the picture. As the story goes, those who have property have earned it through their hard work. Those without property deserve none since they have not worked as hard as those with property. That many people acquire property through inheritance is considered irrelevant.

Political conservatives and libertarians are opposed to all forms of government intervention that might impose restrictions on the use of their private property. Liking things the way they are, they ask no questions about the distribution of income, wealth, education, or property, and are content to leave matters of equity and justice to the marketplace.

For libertarians and others who seek meaning through their individualism, life on a deserted island may be blissful. With no government and no rules on the island, anything goes. You have complete freedom to do whatever you choose with your life on the island. You have no obligations to anyone other than yourself.

The entire island is yours. No one else has any valid claim on the island. Everything is free. You pay no rent and no taxes. Although you have to catch your own fish and trap any game you might eat, the supply of food and water is limitless.

Thou Shalt Not Kill

We have created a world in which people are convinced that it is wrong to kill, unless the nation is threatened because the nation now provides people with a source of ultimate identity, protection, and meaning in life. It is the nation which gives us our "freedom" to be individuals. And since our individual freedom means everything, the nation, as the alleged source of individual freedom becomes our supreme value.

WILLIAM H. WILLIMON[10]

We are quite literally a people that morally live off our wars because they give us the necessary basis for self-sacrifice so that a people who have been taught to pursue only their own interest can at times be mobilized to die for one another. . . . In short, there is nothing wrong with America that a good war cannot cure.

STANLEY HAUERWAS AND
WILLIAM H. WILLIMON[11]

If one's primary concern in life is protecting what one has, then nationalism and patriotism are merely logical extensions of our fixation on private property. For those who have doubts about the meaning of their lives, wrapping themselves in the flag is not an uncommon way of overcoming those self-doubts. "Patriotism is the last refuge of a scoundrel," said Dr. Samuel Johnson. In the blunt words of U.S. Attorney General Ramsey Clark,

> Patriotism as commonly practiced has been a principal cause of war and exploitation. When it proclaims nationalist superiority over others, it is racist. When it compels absolute obedience to government authority, it is fascist. The greatest moral cowardice is obedience to an order to commit an immoral act. When patriotism calls for the use of force to have its way, it becomes criminal. Might does not make right among nations any more than it does among individuals. When patriotism seduces *a* people to celebrate a military slaughter, *the* people have lost their vision.[12]

It is the protection of our cherished individualism which causes the United States to be so bellicose in its foreign policy and to invade tiny countries like Grenada, Libya, Panama, and Iraq.

For centuries before the birth of Christ, people turned to law and reason to deal with meaninglessness. Judaism and Christianity are religions replete with laws and rules of moral conduct which are believed to be derived from God. In many ways, organized religion is evidence of our intellectual, spiritual, and emotional laziness. Rather than a story of our pilgrimage with God, the Bible becomes a book of rules, a means of forsaking the quest by being a substitute for the quest.

Effects of Having

Spiritual	⟶ Orthodoxy
Intellectual	⟶ Hedonism
Emotional	⟶ Narcissism
Physiological	⟶ Health Fetishism

Health Fetishism

Not content with merely having unlimited material possessions, millions of Americans turned their attention in the 1980s to the care and preservation of their own bodies. Indeed, an entire cult evolved focused on physical fitness, body building, and the prolongation of life. On the more conventional side were aerobic exercises, jogging, weight lifting, deep-breathing exercises, and yoga. Health food stores specializing in vitamins, nutrients, designer foods, natural foods, brain stimulants, muscle conditioners, spices, herbs, and aphrodisiacs became increasingly popular. For the vain and narcissistic there were face-lifts, nose jobs, silicone breast implants, and other forms of cosmetic plastic surgery.

Virtual Reality Simulator

*V*irtual Reality Simulator (VRS) provides the ultimate experience in holistic relaxation by stimulating and harmonizing both mental and physiological fitness for sensory rejuvenation and a feeling of homeostasis and well being. Designed to simulate a controlled environment in which your senses of sight, touch, smell, and hearing are subtly integrated to produce a unified effect. VRS combines a vibration massage, a Finnish sauna, a scent-stimulation device, and an audio/visual module to relax your mind through a system of pulsating lights and stereophonic sound. A floating sensation is created by the flow of warm air over the push-button controlled bed. Microprocessor controlled undersurface devices generate pulses which can be adjusted to produce vibration massages. Built-in heat pads soothe aching muscles. The scent-stimulation module comes with four scents—magnolia, bay berry, eucalyptus, and gardenia. Cool scented air aimed at your face has a calming and refreshing effect. The user-friendly VRS control panel allows you to adjust temperature, time, intensity, volume, and vibration continuously. Alternatively, you can use one of the pre-programmed software systems to enhance relaxation, sexuality, weight loss, physical fitness, energy level, creativity, sleep, mental acumen, and longevity. All VRS functions can be monitored on the CRT display. Price: $20,000.

A plethora of physical fitness books appeared promising everything from improved health, mental abilities, and sexual potency to reduced risk of a heart attack, stroke, or cancer. Others claimed to control weight, stimulate the body's immune system, relieve stress and fatigue, and prolong life. And without exception the producers and publishers of these health aids assured consumers that their products were thoroughly grounded in state-of-the-art scientific research.

The latest high-tech life-enhancing device is *virtual reality*. Through virtual reality computers are linked directly to the five body senses so as to create an infinity of other-worldly experiences. If you can't find meaning on your own, virtual reality will enable you to simulate meaning through high-tech sensory mechanisms. Virtual reality video games are now available for children. Who needs marijuana or cocaine, if you can experience virtual reality?

Although good health is of paramount importance to most Americans, others are more concerned with outright survival of any kind of disaster, ranging from blizzards, floods, hurricanes, tornadoes, and earthquakes to nuclear attack. To provide these survival-conscious folk with adequate supplies to meet any unforeseen crisis, an entire industry has been created—the survival industry. Among the supplies offered by these survival companies are emergency food rations, gourmet reserves, portable feminine hygiene items, two-way radios, semi-automatic assault weapons, ammunition cans, grain mills, childbirth kits, gas masks, chemical weapons, and bomb shelters. Survival companies provide strong incentives for those who already have it all to duplicate what they now have. After all, as the reasoning goes,

---

Survival House

*Y*ou have placed yourself in a select group—the group of enlightened individuals who choose to think ahead and prepare for contingencies. You obviously value self-sufficiency and seek to make sure your greatest value—your life—is preserved against whatever factors that may arise to threaten it. You seek to control events rather than let events control you. We offer all the necessary supplies to see you through virtually any crisis.

---

a well-stocked emergency shelter ought to include most of the amenities of one's home.

The Big Lie

But having is obviously not limited to the rich and famous. Many middle-class, blue-collar, and even unemployed Americans also are addicted to shopping malls, Toys "R" Us, high-tech electronics, fancy cars, and credit cards. They too feel the financial and emotional stress of living beyond their means.

In order for our economy to function, those who are expected to do the work must believe in the American dream, which links happiness to what one owns. The path to happiness involves accumulating enough money or credit so that you can buy a nicely furnished home in a good neighborhood, a couple of cars, a color TV, a boat, and a college education for your kids. To be able to afford all these things and eventually pay for them, you must work hard until you retire or die. The harder you work, the more money you will have. The more money you have, the more you can buy, and the happier you will be.

But if this is really true, why are there so many unhappy people in America? Why are the rates of divorce, suicide, abortion, and substance abuse so high, if the American dream is working the way it is supposed to work? As we pointed out earlier, the more we have, the more we want. But once we actually have something, does it make us any happier? Does it give meaning to our life? Again we turn to the philosopher in Ecclesiastes for insight into our malaise.

> Whoever loves money never has money enough;
>> whoever loves wealth is never satisfied with [one's] income.
>> This too is meaningless.
> As goods increase,
>> so do those who consume them.
> And what benefit are they to the owner
>> except to feast [one's] eyes on them? (Eccles. 5:10-11 NIV)

Our entire economy is based on the illusion that the accumulation of wealth and material possessions can provide meaning to life.

The less meaning there is in one's life, the easier it is to be seduced into the materialistic work hard, play hard, be happy syndrome.

To rationalize a political economy driven by meaninglessness and greed, economists have devised powerful myths to convince us that for the good of all to be achieved, it is only necessary for each of us to act egoistically. That is, if consumers, managers, employees, and stockholders all do their own hedonistic thing, their interests will converge in the long run and society will evolve toward some form of socially optimal equilibrium.

Keynes on Having

There is *no* "compact" conferring perpetual rights on those who Have or on those who Acquire. The world is *not* so governed from above that private and social interests always coincide. It is *not* so managed here below that in practice they coincide. It is *not* a correct deduction from the Principles of Economics that enlightened self-interest always operates in the public interest. Nor is it true that self-interest generally is enlightened; more often individuals acting separately to promote their own ends are too ignorant or too weak to attain even these. Experience does *not* show that individuals, when they make up a social unit, are always less clear-sighted than when they act separately.

JOHN MAYNARD KEYNES[13]

The late Joan Robinson once suggested that there had to be a psychological reason for the survival of a thesis which rests on a theory of human nature so thoroughly grounded in nihilism.

There is an irresistible attraction about the concept of equilibrium—the almost silent hum of a perfectly running machine; the apparent stillness of the exact balance of counteracting pressures; the automatic smooth recovery from a chance disturbance. Is there perhaps something Freudian about it? Does it connect with a longing to return to the womb? We have to look for a psychological explanation to account for the powerful influence of an idea that is intellectually unsatisfactory.[14]

The Illusion of Happiness

*E*motions are the essence of humanity. They distinguish us from animals and androids, and bring a meaning to life that often goes unappreciated. But people don't value emotions as they should. The moment they experience an emotion that is discomforting or painful, they attempt to repress or dismiss it, wishing to regain the banality of contentment. This denial of emotion diminishes the human experience. Emotions, after all, are intended to be *felt*, not *overcome*. In *overcoming* them we counteract a natural force. We cease to *live* life, and instead endure it. To endure life is negative. It implies that every action becomes effortful, and that every emotion becomes a burden.

Emotions, no matter how pleasurable or painful, serve an infinite number of purposes. From telling us how to react, to signaling us of misdoing, they constantly inform us of things to be done. Yet unless we experience them with the active mind, we do not become aware of their purposes. We revel blindly in the positive feelings, and endure the negative ones, attempting to weather the trauma unscathed, but no better for our suffering in the end. This is a mistake, for in experiencing them without the active mind, we fail to analyze and interpret them. Their purpose is never disclosed and we have gained nothing from the experience. Emotions, like actions, must be subject to the active mind to become meaningful.

Without the active mind's assistance, we fall prey to the evil of valuing some emotions above others. We embrace the foolish notion that happiness is most meaningful, and that we are entitled to be happy all the time. This idea truly disturbs me, and I have almost reached the point where I disdain happiness. I am not opposed to it, nor am I a masochist. I simply believe that real happiness is the rarest of emotions, and that people are setting too high of an emotional standard when they expect to achieve it continually. In their search for happiness, young people in particular pursue hedonism of all forms, pathetically attempting to drink and adulterate themselves into a state of contentment. In doing so, they mock the every emotion they try to achieve, for the state they attain is not one of happiness, but meaninglessness, the complete negation of the active mind and the spiritual growth of the unconscious.

Happiness, as experienced by the majority of the population, is the ideal of the pigsty, and I condemn it. In acknowledging this, I feel I have rendered my life more meaningful. Unlike others, I am not in pursuit of an illusion. I do not accept happiness as the supreme emotion, and in doing so negate the meaningfulness of all others. I, instead, view all emotions as meaningful, as opportunities to learn about myself, to feel, and grow. Every instant of reality becomes meaningful. I cease to endure and begin to live.

KENDRA HUDSON
First Year Duke Student

But there is nothing new about economists providing the economic underpinnings to support the prevailing ideology. Since the days of Adam Smith, economists have been supplying the rich and the powerful with the kinds of answers they wanted to hear. According to Keynes,

> Practical men, who believe themselves to be quite exempt from any intellectual influences, are usually the slaves of some defunct economist. Madmen in authority, who hear voices in the air, are distilling their frenzy from some academic scribbler of a few years back.[15]

Today it is hardly surprising that few economists feel any discomfort whatsoever in justifying hedonism. Most of the funding for economic research comes from large corporations and the federal government, both of whom have a strong vested interest in promoting greed so that the economy does not collapse. While posing as objective social scientists, all too many economists are willing to sell their souls to the highest bidder.

Ultimately our highly touted way of life, which we believe everyone else in the world should embrace, is deeply rooted in a combination of meaninglessness and the denial of death. It is as though we truly believe that, if we only have enough money, we can buy our own immortality.

Repeated public opinion polls conducted since 1957 suggest that consumerism may not be all that it is cracked up to be. The percentage of Americans claiming to be "very happy" has remained constant over this period at about 33 percent even though personal consumption has doubled.

Our Sole Possession

Although we may accumulate vast sums of money, real estate, financial assets, and material possessions, all of this can be repossessed at any time as a result of wars, civil unrest, theft, natural disasters, national economic catastrophes, incompetence, and eventually death. Ownership is always temporal. Death is the great equalizer. When we die, all our possessions will be distributed by our heirs and the courts. None of our physical possessions is permanent.

What survives? In *The Iliad* of Homer, Odysseus, King of Ithaca, leaves his wife and son to sail away with his army on a military adventure—to rescue Helen of Troy. Ten years of war follow. Ten years after the end of the war, Odysseus and his friends have still not returned home, preferring instead to sail from island to island, engaging in a fantastic series of adventures fighting giants and contending with monsters, gods, and goddesses. The sea god, Poseidon, has it in for Odysseus and places one challenge after another in his way. In good Greek heroic form, Odysseus overcomes every challenge. The tales of these adventures are *The Odyssey*, which, together with *The Iliad*, is one of the great stories of world literature.

Through it all, Odysseus' wife and son wait faithfully at home, with no word of husband and father, Odysseus. Why should Odysseus return home with so many adventures awaiting him on the sea?

The answer comes in Book XI, when Odysseus sails to the very edge of the world and enters the dark regions of Hades, where he meets the shadowy souls of the dead. The Greeks believed that, when we die, we enter a dark, nondescript world of the shades. Odysseus meets all the great Greek heroes from the past. Now, in death, they are as nothing. The dead want only news from the other world, news of friends and family. For Odysseus, his trip to Hades is a confrontation with his own future, an opportunity to put his whole life in perspective. Seeing the emptiness of the state of these departed spirits, Odysseus realizes what is important and unimportant in life. In a symbolic death and rebirth, Odysseus emerges from Hades a different man. He immediately prepares to head for home, to rejoin his wife and son, seeing that this relationship is the only thing that will endure in his life once it is his turn to enter the land of the shadows in Hades.

What endures for us? When we come face-to-face with the end of our lives, the final accounting for who we are, for what we have been, of the roads we have taken and not taken in life, what shall remain?

For Odysseus, it was the legacy of his wife and son; not his heroic exploits and adventures on the sea, but rather the lives of those he influenced and left behind at home. What is our legacy? We know many today who, after a serious accident, during surgery, have had experiences similar to those of Odysseus. They "went to Hades," so to speak. They came face-to-face with their past, and the door was opened on the uncertainty of their future. They came away from the experience changed people.

For too many of us, if we looked back on our lives, we would see little more than an anxious series of accumulated things, a move from this year's "new and improved" car model to the next, the rungs of an unending ladder of acquisitions. Ironically, even as we were accumulating, having, and getting, we were not having. Death is the great thief!

Each of us has a life, now. We may not know what the future holds, nor do we need to know. What we do know is that to each of us has been given the present, our lives, our friends and family, our talents and opportunities. Soul crafting is the point of life, the reason for being. In the end, that is all that remains.

Chapter 5

BEING

Man is what he makes of himself. And the courage to be as oneself is the courage to make of oneself what one wants to be.

PAUL TILLICH
THE COURAGE TO BE

Thus far in our pilgrimage together in search of life's meaning we have encountered three relatively unappealing alternatives— meaninglessness, separation, and having. First, there may be no meaning whatsoever to life. Life may indeed be absurd. Second, life may have meaning, but meaning has eluded us because we are separated from others, ourselves, and the ground of our being. Third, to avoid the pain and suffering associated with meaningless-ness and separation we may seek meaning through having—own-ing, possessing, and controlling money, power, and things. However, as we have seen, having often turns out to be only an illusory source of meaning.

We are left, therefore, with the disquieting conclusion, that if there is any real meaning to life then it is we who must discover it ourselves. Meaning will not be handed to us from on high, but rather we must seek it through *being*—through our creations, our personal relationships, and our experience with pain, suffering, and eventually death. For those of us who have spent our entire lives obsessed with material possessions and wealth, or in the manipulation and control of other people, the realization that we alone are responsible for the creation of our own meaning is sobering. Ralph Waldo Emerson's self-reliant advice, "Trust thyself: every heart vibrates to that iron string,"[1] may seem like cold comfort to a lonely, isolated searcher.

We believe that the search for meaning is primarily concerned with the crafting of our soul—our only possession that can never be taken away even by death. While we are still alive, our soul is who we *are*. It is our *being*—our very essence. Even if there is no life after death on the other side of the mountain, our soul survives as our legacy on earth. At the time of our death, our soul represents the sum of our being. It is the manifestation of who we were and not what we owned or controlled while we were still alive.

The Bible and the Soul

Although the word "soul" has a variety of different meanings in the Bible, it usually signifies the totality of a person. God "breathed the breath of life" into Adam and he became a "living soul" (Gen. 2:7). Soul refers to the unity of the human person—unlike its meaning for the Greeks, who often separated the body from the soul. Soul refers to one's life: Herod sought Jesus' (Matt. 2:20); one might save a soul or take it (Mark 3:4). Death occurs when "God requires your soul" (Luke 12:20).

THE PASTOR

From Jesus Christ, agnostic Albert Camus, psychologist Erich Fromm, atheist Karl Marx, Roman Catholic novelist Walker Percy, theologian Paul Tillich, and psychiatrist Irvin Yalom we hear the message: Life is about being. To live is to be, to have is to die.

Publisher Robert Maxwell and retailer Sam Walton were multibillionaires while they were alive. But now that they are dead, all of their worldly possessions have been distributed. Only their souls remain as evidence of who Robert Maxwell and Sam Walton once were.

Whether we be rich or poor, the only thing over which we have ultimate control is our soul—not in some mystical, metaphysical sense but rather in a very practical sense. If there is life after death on the other side of the mountain, we know not how to influence it. But we do know how to influence the condition of our soul, which survives after death on this side of the mountain, where life has been taken from us.

One's soul is a completely nontransferable asset. It is impossible to own another person's soul, and no one else can control ours.

If our soul is all that we can ever have, how then shall we live our life? Does it make sense to devote so much time and energy to the accumulation of material goods and wealth? Isn't the care and nurturing of our sole possession far more important than having more and more of that which can never be our own? Is it possible to care for our soul alone while ignoring the plight of others—the poor, the needy, the hungry, and the homeless?

Death is the great equalizer in this world. We are all going to die. How will we die? Will we die happy? To die happy we must first live. To live we must be into being. We express our being by creating, loving, caring, sharing, and suffering. In the words of Reinhold Niebuhr,

> Nothing that is worth doing can be achieved in a lifetime; therefore we must be saved by hope. Nothing which is true or beautiful or good makes complete sense in any immediate context of history; therefore we must be saved by faith. Nothing we do, however virtuous, can be accomplished alone. Therefore we are saved by love.[2]

Our Creations

In response to the story of the deserted island, many of the participants in our seminars indicate that in order to avoid going mad, they would build a house, plant a garden, paint the walls of the caves, carve a sculpture out of the rocks, write poetry, or compose music. They would confront the isolation, loneliness, and nonbeing of the island by bringing something new into being—by *creating* something of their own.

But who would benefit from such creations on the island? Is it possible to find meaning from creations which may never be enjoyed by anyone other than the island dweller? Maybe. Maybe not, says Rollo May in *The Courage to Create*. Creativity, according to May, involves discovering "new forms, new symbols, new patterns in which a new society can be built."[3] The realization that one's creations may help form the structure of a new world can be a source of profound joy. But on the island there is no reason to believe there will ever be a new society, since there will be no human beings left after the death of the island's lone inhabitant.

Later in the book, May hints that through one's creations it may still be possible to find meaning on the island even if there are no other people there. He speaks of the passion for form. "It is the struggle against disintegration, the struggle to bring into existence new kinds of being that give harmony and integration."[4] He goes on to say that creative people "do not run away from non-being, but by encountering and wrestling with it, force it to produce being. They knock on silence for an answering music; they pursue meaninglessness until they can force it to mean."[5] "Artistic creation is a demand for unity and a rejection of the world," said Albert Camus.[6] Creation requires courage. Cynical disparaging aloofness is safer than the risk of engagement, search, and creation.

Van Gogh on Creativity

I can very well, in life and in painting, too, do without God. But I cannot, suffering as I do, do without something that is greater than I am, that is my life—the power to create.

VINCENT VAN GOGH[7]

Walt is a craftsman, someone who knows from years of experience, trial and error, testing and learning, how to work with wood. He stood looking at the pile of lumber, sizing up the whole lot of it, surveying it carefully. Then he thrust his hand into the stack of boards, grasping one and withdrawing it. He turned the board over several times, rubbed his hand along the edges, rejected it, and drew forth another. This exercise was repeated with at least a dozen boards. The pieces of wood were touched, turned over, sized up, and rejected. He even smelled them. At last one was judged to be right.

"This one will make up into a table," he pronounced with authoritative conviction. "This one will do fine."

In an age of plastic, stamped out, mass-produced everything, it is a joy to meet someone who has those skills which take time and patience to acquire, standards of judgment and expertise which cannot be bought. Walt's life is obviously better, richer, and more interesting because of his craft, and the lives of others have been enriched by his craftsmanship as well.

We have spoken of soul crafting as the point of life, all that remains after the ravages of time and death. Human beings are animals who eat, reproduce, live, and die. Yet unlike other animals, we also appear to have both a great need and a great ability to create. We are *Homo fabricator,* people who make things. We are rarely content to leave the world as we have found it. While most of our lifetime is consumed with acquiring the basic necessities of life—food, shelter, protection from the elements—we still have some time for leisure. We have surplus energy and time on our hands. We can create.

To carve a whistle, to build a fence, plant a tree, make an apple pie, to paint the ceiling of the Sistine Chapel, to replace the valves on a 1952 Chevrolet—we are often most alive, most ourselves when we are engaged in some act of creativity. Creativity transforms us from a detached observer of life into a responsible participant. So Harold Loukes, a Quaker educator, has asserted, "The young do not need to be preached at; they need to be given a task."

The first book of the Bible, Genesis, tells a story not only of our finitude, the end of life in death, but also of the gift of creativity. As Genesis tells it, God creates us to share in divine creativity:

> Then God said, "Let us make [humankind] in our image, after our likeness; and let them have dominion . . ." So God created [human-kind] in his own image . . . male and female he created them. And God blessed them, and God said to them, "Be fruitful and multiply, and fill the earth and subdue it . . . " And God saw everything that he had made, and behold, it was very good. (Gen. 1:26, 27-28, 31 RSV)

God is here depicted as a master craftsman who creates the woman and the man to share in divine creativity, to create and to craft, mirroring in their own creations some of the exuberance of divine creativity. Although no one is sure just what "in the image of God" means, in the biblical context, it does appear to have something to do with our being co-creators with God.

Creativity is more than simply adding objects to our world (another form of having). From what we have observed, the act of creation is of more consequence in our search for meaning than the thing created. Creativity is not simply throwing blobs of paint on a canvas, or spontaneous outbursts of energy channeled into painting or poetry or wood. Creation involves engagement, discipline, learning skills, mastering technique. The skills and disciplines required to, say, cook a good Cajun meal, are many. The ability to select fresh seafood and vegetables, to know how to control a stove, to know when to add ingredients and how long to cook, are not natural abilities. In fact, one of our students, in telling us how Cajun cooking contributed to meaning in her life, said that it was impossible to cook Cajun without knowing Cajun history and language. One had to, at least through some means of adoption, *be* Cajun.

We live in an age of instant gratification, where people are deceived into thinking that they can buy Cajun food out of a box and prepare it instantly in a microwave. Yet in our better moments we know that good things in life take time—that few worthwhile things are had without effort, without the disciplined submission to the skills and virtues of a craft. Surely the widespread interest in gourmet cooking, arts and crafts, sewing, and other handiwork, is due to many people's realization that we are at our best when we are creating—when we are consciously engaged with the world around us.

As we have seen, many modern jobs are dull, repetitious, uncreative. Our schools continue to crank out students who are adept at spitting back facts and figures on exams and inept at cooking a good meal or making a table, much less playing the violin. Too often, as children, our experiences with art or music, with crafts or writing have served only to convince us that we are not creative, that we can never master the skills required to contribute beauty or pleasure to the world. That means, for many of us, adulthood must be a time for acquiring those skills and disciplines, that freedom and confidence necessary to create.

Our creations remind us that we ought not overly to intellectualize the search for meaning. For most of us, meaning is not found exclusively in books. Few of us live by noble ideas. Rather, we receive meaning from our creations and from the very act of creation. One of our students tried to tell the class why playing the violin gave her life meaning. She told about how, at the end of the day, she was often tired, consumed with many worries and tasks to be done. Yet she habitually took her violin, shut the door to her room, meditated a few minutes, and began to play. She wasn't thinking about giving meaning to her life. In fact, she said that the glory of the playing was that she wasn't thinking about anything more important than the position of her fingers, the movement of the bow on the strings. Mesmerized by the notes of music on the page, utterly absorbed in accomplishing all the physical tasks needed to make music on a violin, she was at peace. Life had meaning and depth. She could go on because of the music.

On Meaning in Poetry

*H*ere, as in life, meaning is, I should say, often more fruit-fully found in the question asked than in any answer given.

ROBERT PENN WARREN
Being Here [8]

In the act of creation, our lives become focused, energy is released, life is given coherence and order. When our creations give others pleasure, we are filled with pride in saying, "I made that." In short, we feel something like God is said to have felt when, surveying us and the world, God pronounced that "behold, it was very good."

Love Relationships

The book of Genesis tells of the creation of humanity in marvel-ously mythic, poetic terms. Having created the man and woman "in the image of God" (Gen. 1:27), God urges them to be creative. They are commanded to "be fruitful and multiply" (Gen. 1:28), to come together and produce children. As someone has said, this surely was the most pleasurable of God's commands! Sex was created by God so that the male and female might participate in divine creativity, saying, "It is not good that the man should be alone"

(Gen. 2:18). Thus the Bible claims that we are created for union and communion with one another, made for love.

For this reason the response of many to life alone on a deserted island is one of sheer horror. For them there could never be meaning on the island without others. Life without love would be nothing. Since there are no other people with whom to form personal relationships, one might turn to God or nature. But could such one-way relationships be sustained? What kind of feedback could there be? Is it possible to have love without two-way interaction?

Nowhere is the case for love expressed more eloquently than in Paul's letter to the Corinthians:

> If I speak in the tongues of men and of angels, but have not love, I am a noisy gong or a clanging cymbal. And if I have prophetic powers, and understand all mysteries and all knowledge, and if I have all faith, so as to remove mountains, but have not love, I am nothing. If I give away all I have, and if I deliver my body to be burned, but have not love, I gain nothing.

> Love is patient and kind; love is not jealous or boastful; it is not arrogant or rude. Love does not insist on its own way; it is not irritable or resentful; it does not rejoice at wrong, but rejoices in the right. Love bears all things, believes all things, hopes all things, endures all things.

> Love never ends; as for prophecies, they will pass away; as for tongues, they will cease; as for knowledge, it will pass away. For our knowledge is imperfect and our prophecy is imperfect; but when the perfect comes, the imperfect will pass away. When I was a child, I spoke like a child, I thought like a child, I reasoned like a child; when I became a man, I gave up childish ways. For now we see in a mirror dimly, but then face to face. Now I know in part; then I shall understand fully, even as I have been fully understood. So faith, hope, love abide, these three; but the greatest of these is love.

> (1 Corinthians 13 RSV)

In *The Road Less Traveled,* psychiatrist M. Scott Peck defined love as "the will to extend one's self for the purpose of nurturing one's own or another's spiritual growth."[9] Theologian Paul Tillich spoke of love as a sort of innate energy by which we are driven to overcome our separation and to move toward unity. This drive toward union may be expressed in sexual desire, friendship, and many ways through which we give ourselves to others. Augustine said that love drives us toward God: "Our hearts are restless till they find their rest in thee" (*Confessions,* book 7).

Yet love is not an unconflicted human disposition. Most of the wonderful things we do, we do for love. Paradoxically, most of the really dreadful things we do to one another are also often attributed to love. Even though few of us would think about murdering another person, many of us are willing to kill other people because we love our nation. Domestic violence, spouse abuse, abuse of our elders and our children are all testimony to our ability to inflict terrible pain upon those we love.

Each of us knows from personal experience the superficiality of the phrase "love is all you need." Love is rarely without conflict, hardly ever completely selfless and self-giving toward the other. The human drive toward having and possessing can be expressed subtly but powerfully in love. Freud believed that all human actions, even those which appear to be completely self-giving and loving, are only different ways of gaining pleasure for the self. Pure love is only an illusion, according to Freud. There is no love which is not simply another form of self-love.

Psychotherapist Erich Fromm challenges Freud's suspicion of our motives for loving in books like *The Art of Loving.*[10] Building on Jesus' command to love the neighbor *as* the self, Fromm argues that concern for the self need not necessarily be selfish. Fromm sees selfish people in what we have called the "having mode." The selfish person, far from loving the self, has so little self-love that he or she must compensate for lack of self-respect through anxious accumulation of things. Only as one truly respects oneself, truly loves oneself, can one truly let go of oneself long enough to love and respect others.

Because the words "I love you" may really mean "I love me and want to use you to love me even more," love can be dangerous, full of opportunity for self-deception. That is one reason why most religions and societies urge couples to test their love through public promises—marriage. Yet because we do appear to be driven toward union—sexual, emotional, intellectual, spiritual—we keep falling in love, keep bonding with one another. In love, we rise above ourselves, move beyond ourselves, and find that our being, which for much of our lives was our sole concern, is suddenly tied up with someone else whom we love. To have only ourselves to love, to have no greater project in life than ourselves, is surely the very depths of meaninglessness. Conversely, to be in love with another is to find yourself considerably and delightfully enlarged from an *I* into a *we*. Our world is larger, which may be one reason why, when we are very much in love with another person, the whole world seems much more lovely and lovable.

Loneliness and Love

To fully relate to another, one must first relate to oneself. If we cannot embrace our own aloneness, we will simply use the other as a shield against isolation. Only when one can live like the eagle—with no audience whatsoever—can one turn to another in love; only then is one able to care about the enlargement of the other's being.[11]

IRVIN D. YALOM
When Nietzsche Wept

Even though there are plenty of reasons for us to behave in a purely selfish fashion, we are capable of amazingly selfless acts of altruism and self-sacrifice for others. Most of us, though we may be reluctant to claim that we are the best exemplars of pure love for others, have been the beneficiaries of such love. In the next chapter, when we ask you to list your personal objectives in life, you are almost certain to list some form of loving relationship. Whether as friends, lovers, husbands, or wives—our giving and receiving of love make most of our lives worth living. It does appear that our hearts are restless, and they do not rest until they rest in the giving and receiving of love with another—a view expressed quite poignantly by Leah de Roulet:

If there is a real purpose for any of us, it is to somehow enhance each other's humanity—to love, to touch others' lives, to put others in touch with basic human emotions, to know that you have made even one life breathe easier because you have lived.[12]

Shakespeare on Love

*L*et me not to the marriage of true minds
Admit impediments. Love is not love
Which alters when it alteration finds,
Or bends with the remover to remove:
Oh, no! it is an ever-fixed mark,
That looks on tempests and is never shaken;
It is the star to every wandering bark,
Whose worth's unknown, although his height be taken.
Love's not Time's fool, though rosy lips and cheeks
Within his bending sickle's compass come:
Love alters not with his brief hours and weeks,
But bears it out even to the edge of doom.
If this be error and upon me proved,
I never writ, nor no man ever loved.

Sonnet 116

More will be said about our longing for human connectedness and community in chapter 7.

Pain and Suffering

On the face of it, pain and suffering might seem like topics more appropriate for our discussion of meaninglessness and separation than as sources of meaning. In the biblical book of Job, Job found no meaning in his suffering and loss. After losing his family, his goods, his health, Job said,

> Let the day perish wherein I was born. . . .Why did I not die at birth, come forth from the womb and expire? . . . Or why was I not buried like a stillborn child? . . . Why is light given to one in misery, and life to the bitter in soul, who long for death, but it does not come?
> (Job 3:3, 11, 16, 20-21 RSV, adapted)

Pain and suffering may be seen as precursors of death, a foretaste of what it is like to be nothing. Physical pain is a nasty reminder that we are animals, that we suffer, grow old, die. Often, in our suffering, we feel a terrible sense of isolation. The world passes us by and few really seem able to feel as bad as we feel. Most of modern life appears utterly committed to the proposition that suffering is an unmitigated evil to be avoided or drugged away at any cost. Pain is evidence that somehow our drugs or our systems of social support have failed. Some fundamentalist preachers blame AIDS on sexual promiscuity among gay people, and gay rights groups blame AIDS on lack of government funding. Both groups seem shocked by what ought to be—considering everything we know about human life— an obvious fact of life; namely, that *life is suffering and pain.*

But again, why focus on that somber truth here, in the search for meaning? Somewhat surprisingly, pain and suffering are not only unavoidable aspects of life, but also potential sources of life's meaning as well.

When queried about survival on the deserted island, a young woman in our Duke seminar responded that she would seek meaning on the island by confronting the isolation and loneliness of the island—by attempting to rise above the pain and suffering imposed on her by fate. She felt that meaning could be found by attempting to beat the odds, so to speak, of survival alone on the island.

Our culture has managed to empty suffering of meaning. About all we are taught to feel—when it comes our turn to be in pain or to suffer because of life's circumstances—is resentment. And yet, picture a world without suffering and pain. Of course, it would be a fantasy world, a world we have never known, but we presume that it would be a wonderful world. Imagine a world without the pain of hunger, thirst, heat, cold, disease.

Yet it would also be a world without much human creativity or purpose either. So many of humanity's greatest achievements would be pointless in such a world. What would be the need of agriculture, architecture, or care for others in such a world? A hedonistic paradise would have no need for human creativity or ingenuity because there would be no difficulties to be overcome or problems to be solved, no need for human cooperation. In short, the world would be perfectly pleasurable but utterly inhuman.

We are not machines. We are therefore not anesthetized creatures who feel nothing. My actions toward you are of consequence. I am capable not only of feeling but also of inflicting great pain; therefore, the question of my morality becomes a big question indeed.

Yet we ought not to speak too positively about pain. Not all pain has adaptive significance. Because of disastrous health conditions, some 14.5 million children die each year before the age of five mostly in impoverished countries such as Bangladesh, Ethiopia, Mozambique, and Somalia. For hundreds of millions of people, meaning is defined in terms of the pain and suffering of raw survival. When one has added up all the pain in the world, made allowances for that pain which has spurred us on toward invention and achievement, toward community and responsibility, there is still far too much pain left over for us to be too positive about the potential meaningfulness of pain.

However, we have all known people whose pain appeared to make rather than break them. It is perhaps one of the noblest aspects of the human spirit that we have the ability to wrench meaning out of even something so potentially debilitating as pain and suffering. Nietzsche's great maxim, "That which does not destroy me strengthens me," is exemplified in the lives of many who have lived their lives with such meaning that what we might label a "handicap" has, in the way they have crafted their souls, been transformed into a gift. How does that happen?

A childbirth is said to be about as painful as a kidney stone, yet, most of the time, it is experienced as far less painful. A battlefield doctor noticed that injuries received in battle appeared to be far less painful for the recipient than the same injuries suffered in a car accident. Why? Suffering is more than a physical sensation. Pain is not in itself very interesting. What is interesting is that we appear to have the capacity to find meaning in pain and, in finding meaning in even the worst pain, the pain is not so painful.

In her book, *I Hope*, Raisa Gorbachev emphasized the tragic role pain and suffering have played in shaping Russian history and in defining the sense of meaning of the Russian people. Poignantly she said, "The most important thing that my parents gave me was a capacity to share other people's needs and to enter into their grief, their pain: the quality of empathy. . . . No, not a single generation lives in vain on this sinful earth."[14]

The Pain and Suffering of Russian Women

It was in the depths of the country that I experienced again the living pain of war, the sad aura of which still enshrouded the nation's life, although it was already twenty years since the war ended. . . . Can you imagine it? A woman who has lost everything, whose life was literally destroyed by the war. . . . Women who had never known the happiness of love or the joy of motherhood. Women living out their lives alone in old, tumbledown houses that were also at the end of their days. If you think about it, we are talking about people whom nature intended to be the givers of life and to be at its center. And it was amazing to find that the majority of those women had not become bitter, did not hate the whole world and had not withdrawn into themselves, but had preserved the selflessness and the sympathy for the misfortunes and sorrows of others that have always animated the Russian woman's heart. It is really amazing!

RAISA M. GORBACHEV
I Hope[13]

Meaning arising out of something as apparently meaningless as pain has to be life's great paradox. While few of us will join those who speak of pain, particularly someone else's pain, as "God's will," many can attest that their suffering has produced in them patience, gratitude for life, empathy with other sufferers, or other positive benefits.

In *Man's Search for Meaning*, Viktor Frankl, who, as a prisoner of the Nazis, certainly knew pain on a scale few of us will ever be asked to endure, claimed, "Suffering ceases to be suffering at the moment it finds a meaning."[15] Frankl recounts how he was able to keep going, to surprise even himself with his ability to endure extreme deprivation and hardship in the death camp, because he kept thinking of his family, kept composing in his mind a book he had been working on before his imprisonment.

Reading Frankl's account of his time at the camp (and we do recommend that you read it), one realizes that Frankl did not discover meaning at the camp, as if his life was only waiting for a particularly horrible period of pain to teach him important lessons. Frankl's experience is interesting in what he brought to the camp. His resilient conviction that life, even in its worst moments, has meaning, that he himself had charge over his destiny, even while his Nazi guards thought they were robbing him of any shred of human hope and dignity, all served Frankl well in the camp. So perhaps the lesson to be learned from an account of meaning within suffering like *Man's Search for Meaning* is that it is not pain which has meaning but what we bring to our pain that gives it meaning.

To find meaning in life, even amid terrible pain and suffering, has to be the ultimate testimony to the resilience of the human spirit, a challenge to the rest of us who are not in pain or suffering at the moment so to craft our lives that, when it comes our turn to suffer, to be in mental or physical anguish, we shall be able to find meaning even there.

Is There Any Other Way to Live?

When compared with the other three stages of meaning—meaninglessness, separation, and having, why are so few people attracted to being as a way to live their lives? Being is a high-risk but potentially high-return life-style. Some people simply are not very creative. Creativity is not an act of will alone. Second, it is quite possible to fail at love and personal relationships. Fear of rejection prevents many of us from reaching out to others. Although we all long for some sense of community with other people, few of us have

Sighing for Eden—Sin, Evil, and the Christian Faith

The problem is not simply pain, that we feel pain, or that some pain is too much—but that we find so little meaning in some pain.

Anguish is the concomitant of meaningless pain. It divides the pain of childbirth from the pain of cancer. It often afflicts people who are not in physical pain. In affluent, prosperous countries, why are so many people driven to drug addiction, marital stress, and suicide? As a pastor, I find the anguish caused in a family because of an alcoholic to be a greater challenge to my faith and theirs than the anguish caused when someone in a family has terminal cancer. Some of the most intense, complex suffering appears to be nonphysical, the result of anguish caused by meaninglessness . . .

The problem, it seems to me, is not that suffering and pain exist in the world and that we feel them. The real problem is that suffering seems so random and so meaningless, crushing people as often as it ennobles them, falling upon the undeserving and deserving alike.

We must reject any response which rationalizes someone's misery by saying, "You suffer because you have been bad and deserve to suffer" or "This suffering is God's will." That would be to call evil good.

Suffering and pain, particularly in their undeserved, excessive, and chronic forms, are an awesome mystery. Suffering falls with a kind of haphazardness and inequality on people. It is often incredibly unfair, a great mystery among other mysteries which remind us that there is always a "beyond" in even our best and most reasoned explications of the world.

Pain is so threatening to us, in part, because it is the ultimate challenge to our self-idolatry: The accusing, relentless forewarning of our ever-impending death. It produces anxiety because it is a concrete, unavoidable reminder that we are frail, physical creatures who shall die. Like any reminder of our finitude, pain presents us with the opportunity either to turn aside into fantasy, false hope, or despair, or else to turn toward God.

THE PASTOR

Humor in the Search

$\mathcal{W}$here to put humor as a means of creatively dealing with meaninglessness? Surely it belongs in our discussion of *being*, an integral part of our creativity, our relationships, and intelligent response to pain and suffering. The cultivation of and delight in humor is an experience of ourselves at our best. Through humor, we laugh to keep from crying, we rise above our immediate circumstances, we impudently refuse to keep silence, to acquiesce to life's tragedies. No wonder some of our best comedians are African Americans, Jews, the poor people who actually know, from personal experience, what injustice feels like, how those in power exercise their power at others' expense. Through humor, we thumb our noses at tyrants and demagogues, we laugh through our tears, we lay hold of life in a manner which is playful, creative, and not morbid, self-pitying, or nihilistic.

Where humor comes from, we do not know. Yet we do know that humor has much to do with the search for meaning. When we laugh, we usually laugh at life's incongruities. Our laughter implies an innate conviction that life is supposed to have purpose, direction, meaning. When it does not, we laugh. When we laugh, we are busy working with the realities of life, refashioning them, rising above them, on our way to transcendence.

Thus, when one of our students stated, in his goals and objectives, his intention, "To find a fit subject for marriage and to marry her by the time I am twenty-eight," we laughed. Of course, he was supposed to be setting goals, but love and marriage stated in this manner seemed funny. We pictured his coming up to a young woman at a party and saying to her, "Hello, you look like a fit subject for marriage."

Mark Twain said, "Everything human is pathetic. The secret source of Humor itself is not joy but sorrow. There is no humor in heaven."

There is humor in the search for meaning. Especially there.

THE PASTOR

Effects of Being

Spiritual   ⟶   Quest
Intellectual   ⟶   Growth
Emotional   ⟶   Balance
Physiological ⟶   Homeostasis

---

ever experienced real community—the subject of chapter 7. Last, our tolerance for pain and suffering is so low that neither could ever be a source of meaning.

But while the risks associated with being are very high, the fourth column of the life matrix discussed in chapter 1 suggests that the payoffs from being very often outweigh the risks. Being can lead to spiritual quest, intellectual growth, emotional balance, and physiological homeostasis. Homeostasis refers to the condition which exists when the interdependent elements and functions of the human body are in a state of relatively stable equilibrium. In no sense are we suggesting that being is a physiological cure-all for all ailments. Rather what we are saying is that there is a better chance for body, mind, and soul to work together in the being mode than is often the case in the having mode. If there is a hearing impairment or a heart problem for example, then the mind and body work together to compensate for the problem rather than pretend the problem doesn't exist. As our body ages, we must adjust the spiritual, intellectual, and emotional dimensions of our life. Those into being seem to find these transitions to be more natural and less threatening.

Psychotherapy and Being

The whole purpose of psychotherapy is to teach the patient how to be.

THE PSYCHIATRIST

Regardless of one's opinion of Christianity as a religion, the story of Jesus Christ is a story about someone who was into being—loving, caring, sharing, healing, suffering, and dying on the cross.

A *Time* magazine cover story on the simple life called it a "revolution in progress" and suggested that Americans may be ripe for such insights. "In place of materialism," the story declared, "many Americans are embracing simpler pleasures and homier values. They've been thinking hard about what really matters in their lives, and they've decided to make some changes. What matters is having time for family and friends, rest and recreation, good deeds and spirituality. . . . The pursuit of a simpler life with deeper meaning is a major shift in America's private agenda."[16]

Two writers who walked away from the fast track of Los Angeles screenplays and journalism respectively are Frank Levering and Wanda Urbanska. In their book *Simple Living*, Frank and Wanda describe how they grew weary of having it all and decided to leave the clutter of Southern California in favor of a simpler life running the family orchard in the Blue Ridge Mountains of Virginia. Through numerous examples, such as choosing to maintain an old American car rather than buy a new one, they teach us how to be. Many of their examples are equally applicable to those of us who are not fortunate enough to live in a Blue Ridge orchard.[17]

In *Groundhog Day*, the movie mentioned in chapter 2, TV weatherman Bill Murray is able to move beyond February 2 only when he rids himself of his selfish, egocentric ways, gives a beggar a hundred-dollar bill, helps some old ladies along the highway, takes up the piano, and relates to his girlfriend in a loving, caring way. Murray's life becomes more meaningful when he lapses into being.

The transition from having to being is not an easy one for most of us. We are so accustomed to the old ways that having seems almost natural. After surviving open-heart surgery, a middle-aged accountant denounced his life of having and proclaimed his commitment to being. "But it's very difficult," he said. "My friends think I'm a little strange and don't seem to understand why I want to spend more time with my family and less time working and acquiring." Those who conform to the social status quo feel threatened by those who attempt to break free. In our fast-paced, consumer-driven society, we have to pay a high price to be. But it's worth it!

A Searcher's Prayer

*D*ear God, teach me how to be!

Chapter 6

THE PERSONAL SEARCH

Is there any meaning in my life which will not be destroyed by the inevitable death awaiting me?

LEO TOLSTOY
MY CONFESSION, MY RELIGION, THE GOSPEL IN BRIEF

Despite our warnings to the contrary, many of the participants in our seminars and workshops come to us with the expectation that they will be provided with meaning kits at the end of the course, which will reveal the true meaning of life. They are looking for a quick-fix for their pain, and "the Search for Meaning" seems to have a nice ring to it. Dozens of pop psychology books published in the 1980s by various gurus and spiritual counselors assured us that there is no pain or confusion in life that cannot be quickly cured in three easy steps. Many fundamentalist TV evangelists have promised the same.

But there is nothing easy about the search for meaning. Even as life is full of pain and difficulty, so too is the search. We cannot promise that, if one follows our process, a meaning light will suddenly appear at the end of the tunnel revealing all. The quest for meaning involves discipline, soul searching, and just plain hard work. For this reason, three of the seven steps of the search process outlined in chapter 1 involve very specific written exercises. They include:

1. personal history
2. personal philosophy
3. personal strategic plan

For these exercises to be effective and to contribute to our search, they must be approached with a dogged commitment to introspection and the realization that what we write could have profound influence over the rest of our life. We only live once. Doesn't it make sense to pay close attention to what is going on in our life and to what we want in the future? What happened in the past is non-negotiable and can never be changed. The clock is running. But we can help shape our own future.

Ten Questions for Our Search

1. Who am I?
2. Where am I going?
3. How can I prevent my life from being a series of accidents?
4. What do I want to be when I grow up?
5. How shall I overcome my separation from others, myself, and the ground of my being?
6. What shall I do to resist the temptation to have?
7. How does one learn how to be?
8. Can I find meaningful employment?
9. Is it possible to experience real community?
10. How can I die happy?

Life History

First, we take note of where we have been before committing to the search. This involves writing a short history of what we consider to be the most meaningful events in our life. Such a history need not be more than five pages, but it should attempt to capture those occurrences in our life which we feel have given us meaning: personal encounters, the death of a loved one, a great disappointment, the achievement of an important objective, the birth of a child, a poignant conversation, or the viewing of a work of art or one of the wonders of nature.

Writing a *personal history* is not an easy task—particularly if our past is full of unpleasant events about which we prefer not to be reminded. Those who have been severely abused physically, sexually, or mentally may find it virtually impossible to write a personal history without professional assistance. Indeed, one of the principal objectives of psychotherapy is to help the patient narrate his or her past. If your history is difficult to recall, try writing a letter to yourself or your parent describing the past. Take a walk in the woods using a hand-held recorder and freely associate on your past.

It is unimportant that the events recorded in our personal history be in chronological order. What is important is that we be honest about our interpretation of the significance of these events. A thoughtful personal history can provide the grounding and frame of reference for writing our personal philosophy and strategy. It represents an inventory of all that has been meaningful in our life.

There may be a risk in writing our personal history. Consideration of our past reminds us that many aspects of our life are rooted in meaninglessness. Indeed, the writing of such an essay may give credence to the view that life is absurd. One of our students, in writing his personal history, realized that during most of his life, nearly all his free time had been spent on his sofa, watching TV. It was a devastating realization. The quest for meaning often involves a plunge into a sea of nothingness. But we will never discover meaning if we cannot first find the courage to confront our own meaninglessness and death.

Personal Philosophy

If our personal history has been carefully prepared, it can be used to undertake the next two exercises: our *personal philosophy* and *personal strategy*. A personal philosophy is a declaration of first principles by which we live our lives. Such a philosophy attempts to state the essence of who we are at the core of our existence. If carefully done, it defines the ground of our being and represents a snapshot of our soul.

Everyone has a personal philosophy. However, few of us take the time to draft our philosophy on a sheet of paper. As painful and difficult as it may be, drafting our philosophy can bring a certain degree of discipline to the search process. An unwillingness to write our thoughts on paper may reflect our fear of finding out who we are and what we are about.

A personal philosophy contains four interdependent elements:

1. sense of meaning
2. statement of values
3. ethics
4. statement of social responsibility

Obviously, if we have no *sense of meaning,* then formulating a personal philosophy is impossible. But the very act of trying to write such a piece may help us come to terms with our existential anxieties and meaninglessness. Arguably there is meaning in the search itself, and writing is a critical part of the search process.

A useful beginning often involves compiling a shoot-from-the-hip list of possible sources of meaning starting with those events in our life which were included in our personal history. We may also want to give serious consideration to the four columns of the life matrix described in chapter 1—meaninglessness, separation, having, and being. From an initial exhaustive list of meaning options we can then pare down the list so that it includes only those activities and events which are *most* meaningful to us. Looking at this list, write a statement about what means most to you. It goes without saying, that the development of a sense of meaning is a continuous evolution. In the early stages of our quest, anything that we write should be viewed as tentative and subject to revision as we experience life with all of its uncertainties. Our statement of personal philosophy may provide an effective frame of reference around which to organize our search.

Once we have made at least an initial effort to formulate a statement of our sense of meaning, we may turn our attention to formulating a set of personal *values.* Values are social principles or standards by which we judge ourselves. Our values are strongly influenced by our sense of meaning and vice versa.

Our values should reflect the importance of the spiritual, intellectual, emotional, and physiological dimensions of our life as noted in the life matrix. Among the values that often appear in statements of values are justice, equality, liberty, love, efficiency, fidelity, loyalty, gratitude, beneficence, and self-improvement. If our values are consistent with our sense of meaning, then they can be used as a way of checking up on ourselves as we pursue our search for meaning. That is, if our behavior is clearly inconsistent with our values, then we may want to either change our behavior or consider the possibility of reformulating our sense of meaning and adjusting our values accordingly. Later, when we write our personal strategy, it will be instructive to look for incongruities between our stated values and our planned strategies.

Not unlike our sense of meaning, the compiling of a statement of values is also an evolutionary undertaking. We may begin by producing a long list of, say, fifteen to twenty possible values. Some of these values may be either redundant, inconsistent with each other, or incompatible with our sense of meaning, and can therefore be deleted from our list. Our final list of values should probably contain no more than five or six values to which we are seriously committed. We believe that it is far more prudent to have a short list of values in which we truly believe, than to have a long list which allows us to pretend to be all things to all people but unfaithful to ourselves.

Our choice of values and our sense of meaning get right to the heart of the matter. They are statements about how we intend to nurture our soul, about the person we intend to be in life. Our personal philosophy is our blueprint for crafting our soul.

Ethics is a picture of what constitutes moral or immoral human conduct. What constitutes ethical or unethical behavior depends on our sense of meaning, our character, our habits, our virtues, and our personal values. Vincent Barry has summarized some ethical principles in his book *Moral Issues in Business,* some of which are outlined below: Clearly, our choice of ethical principles will be shaped by our personal experiences, religious beliefs, and education.

Unfortunately, ethical principles are often rigid, inflexible, and difficult to apply. For example, in a life-threatening situation, how would we use the Golden Rule to decide whether to save our spouse, our child, or some unrelated person, if only one of them could be saved? Most of us are as concerned with the ultimate results of our behavior as we are concerned about the originating principles for our actions.

Ethical Principle	Rule of Conduct
1. *Egoism*	Promote the individual's best long-term interests.
2. *Utilitarianism*	Produce the greatest ratio of good to evil for everyone.
3. *Situational Ethics*	Produce the greatest amount of Christian love.
4. *Golden Rule*	Do unto others as you would have them do unto you.
5. *Categorical Imperative*	Behave in such a way that you wish the maxim of your action to be a universal law.
6. *Liberty Rule*	People in the original position would expect each person participating in a practice or affected by it to have an equal right to the greatest amount of liberty that is compatible with a like liberty for all.[1]

Laura L. Nash has come up with an interesting alternative to ethical principles for addressing ethical business decisions, which may be applicable to many nonbusiness decisions as well. She has suggested twelve questions to aid managers in making tough ethical decisions:

1. Have you defined the problem accurately?
2. How would you define the problem if you stood on the other side of the fence?
3. How did this situation occur in the first place?
4. To whom and to what do you give your loyalty as a per-person and as a member of the corporation?
5. What is your intention in making the decision?
6. How does this intention compare with the probable results?
7. Whom could your decision or action injure?
8. Can you discuss the problem with the affected parties before you make your decision?

9. Are you confident that your position will be as valid over a long period of time as it seems now?
10. Could you disclose without qualm your decision or action to your boss, your CEO, the board of directors, your family, society as a whole?
11. What is the symbolic potential of your action if understood? If misunderstood?
12. Under what conditions would you allow exceptions to your stand?[2]

Although the application of Nash's twelve questions to nonbusiness ethical dilemmas may appear to be simplistic, it provides us a great deal of information on which to base our decisions. The process of answering these questions may very well be more important than the answers to the questions themselves.

The American Catholic bishops have proposed three questions for evaluating national economic policies, which have applicability far beyond the national economy. The questions are: What does the policy do for people? What does it do to people? How do people participate in its implementation? These same questions are relevant to decisions affecting business enterprises, educational institutions, hospitals, churches and synagogues, governments, and even families. Regardless of one's political ideology, it's hard to find fault with the applicability of these questions to a broad range of ethical issues. For those looking for pinpoint precision in their search for rules of ethical conduct, the bishops' three questions may be woefully inadequate, but they have the value of pointing us toward the results of our actions as much as toward their origins.

One weakness of approaching the *personal philosophy* in this way—listing values, describing ethics as a series of questions, as a problem of gathering inadequate information—is that we make values, principles, a philosophy of life sound detached, abstracted from who we are as people. Life is more than a series of detached ethical quandaries. As we decide and act, our soul is being crafted. Most of us are more complex than merely individuals who subscribe to certain "values." We have character, we are individuals with a history, a web of commitments, visions, and habits. Perhaps it would be better to list the virtues we hope to cultivate in ourselves than the values we think we hold. Who do we hope to resemble by the time we are seventy?

Try, therefore, in describing your personal philosophy, to describe who you are (and hope one day to be) at your best. Our personal philosophy is more than a shopping list of abstract, admirable virtues. Rather, it is a description of those habits, commitments, moral visions, and cultivated virtues that make you a coherent, whole, worthwhile person.

Given a set of values and ethical principles, a sketch of our character, how do we apply them to our parents, relatives, spouse, children, friends, enemies, colleagues, government, and society as a whole? That is the aim of a statement of *social responsibility*. Such a statement attempts to sort out the relative priority we assign to different people with whom we have either direct or indirect contact. Are we concerned only with the members of our immediate family and local community? What sense of responsibility do we feel for those less fortunate than ourselves who live in Africa, Asia, or Latin America? Can we find meaning if we pretend that we live on a deserted island where we are responsible only to ourselves?

In contrast to the 1960s when many Americans were genuinely concerned with the welfare of minorities, the poor, and the disadvantaged, in the 1980s our attention turned inward toward ourselves and our immediate family. As Robert Bellah pointed out in *Habits of the Heart,* our attention shifted away from social and community values toward individualism and so-called family values. Concern for communal and social values was equated with socialism and was to be avoided at all cost.

As we work our way through the elements of our personal philosophy, we should make frequent reference to the states of meaning outlined in the life matrix in chapter 1 and described in more detail in chapters 2 through 5. To what extent is our life subsumed by meaninglessness and separation? Have we drifted by default into a life of having? Do we have the courage to define our own meaning, values, ethics, and social responsibility? Is our philosophy our very own, or is it an attempt to impress or please a false self, a parent, a child, a spouse, a friend, a priest, or a god?

Personal Strategy

Our personal history essay described where we have been in our search. Our personal philosophy spelled out who we are. The next question is, What do we want to be when we grow up? This leads us to the third written exercise in our search process—the formulation of a *personal strategic plan.*

Planning

*P*lanning will never become an exact science.
But it now can be less of a venture into the unknown.
The future is a moving target.
Planning can improve our aim.

IBM

A strategic plan is a blueprint of the big picture of our life, which we can follow as we pursue our search for life's meaning. Just as many corporate managers have found it useful to formulate a long-term strategic business plan, we too may benefit from a similar plan applied to our own life. It is close to the "map" recommended by M. Scott Peck.

The objective of personal strategic planning is to provide us with a process that will enable us to make decisions today that will affect the spiritual, intellectual, emotional, and physiological dimensions of our life in the future and to do so in an environment characterized by a high degree of risk and uncertainty. Personal strategic planning involves the formulation, analysis, and implementation of a set of personal strategies aimed at achieving our long-term goals and objectives in light of our personal strengths and weaknesses and a set of assumptions about our external environment.

Fearing a loss of control over their lives, many people have a strong aversion to any form of planning. But this is an incorrect perception. Planning actually enables us to increase the degree of control we have over our life by anticipating uncertain personal, economic, and political events while we are still in a position to influence their impact on our life. Others avoid planning because they are embarrassed by the shallowness of their objectives, which becomes painfully obvious when plans are expressed in black and white.

The personal strategic planning process consists of the following five elements.

1. external environment
2. situation assessment
3. objectives
4. goals
5. strategies

We begin the strategic planning process with a forecast—preferably a multiscenario forecast—of the principal *external forces* likely to have an impact on our life over the next ten years. These might include personal, family, economic, political, social, cultural, and environmental forces. Some people find it useful to include optimistic, pessimistic, and "most likely" scenarios for these external forces. Others have a tendency to assume that whatever is happening today in their external environment will continue for the foreseeable future. Rarely is this the case. For example, MBA students at Duke University's Fuqua School of Business in the 1980s always assumed in their personal strategic plans that the economic prosperity of the Reagan years would continue unabated forever.

What we try to accomplish with an external environmental forecast is a reasonable stab at where the world is going over the next decade. Will we have a stable family life? Will the country be at war or will it enjoy peace and prosperity? Will there be steady economic growth or erratic fluctuations in the economy? Will life

---

Yalom on Personal Planning

Not to take possession of your life plan is to let your existence be an accident.

IRVIN D. YALOM
When Nietzsche Wept[3]

become simpler or even more complex than it is today? Will the pattern of violence continue?

Then with an eye on our personal history and our statement of philosophy, we attempt to assess our *situation,* our own personal strengths and weaknesses. What are our assets and what are our liabilities? What do we bring to the table, so to speak? Although few of us have difficulty enumerating our virtues, facing up to our shortcomings is more painful. Honesty is particularly important in this stage of the strategic planning process.

Returning briefly to our discussion of freedom and destiny in chapter 3, the external environment and our strengths and weaknesses are the givens in our life. They represent our fate. At least in the short run, we have limited ability to alter either our external environment or our personal qualities. However, over the long run we may be able to make some adjustments in our character and confront some aspects of our external environment such as our family or the local political situation.

Personal *objectives* are generated statements of the direction in which we want to go with our life over the long run in light of our personal philosophy, our strengths and weaknesses, and our forecast of the external environment. They represent a desired future state of being toward which we want to strive. Objectives are usually descriptive rather than quantitative and do not have target completion dates associated with them. Examples of personal objectives include: To have a fulfilling marriage. To achieve financial independence. To die happy. With our objectives, we are attempting to gain the freedom to turn our fate into our destiny.

Personal *goals,* on the other hand, are much more specific than objectives. They refer to a specific achievement to be realized within a definite period of time. Goals are often quantifiable. Whether or not we are prepared to commit to specific numerical targets and dates associated with them is strong evidence of the degree of our commitment to personal strategic planning. A personal plan that contains no specific goals to be accomplished within a specific time horizon is a sham, a waste of time and energy. Goals are bench marks on the way to meeting an objective. A goal might be to find a partner suitable for marriage within two years. Another goal might be to achieve a certain level of income or financial net worth by a designated date. Graduation from law school or medical school by the age of thirty also could be a goal. Clearly, spiritual and emotional goals are more difficult to articulate than financial and professional goals.

Goals represent measures of performance by which we judge our progress in achieving our objectives. For example, financial stability may be our objective, but an income level of $80,000 a year by the time we are forty may be our goal. To meet the objective of a happy family life with our children, we may pursue a long-term marriage goal.

Whether or not we achieve our personal goals and objectives depends on the external environment, our strengths and our weaknesses, and the actions we take to get what we want. These actions are called *strategies*. A strategy is a collection of activities aimed at achieving our goals and objectives. How we spend our time, money, or any other resource is a strategy.

It is very common for people to confuse strategies with goals and objectives. For example, buying a vacation house is a strategy—an action. Accumulating enough money to buy a $150,000 vacation house is a goal. Applying for admission to graduate school is also a strategy. Completing a Ph.D. is a goal. Going to church, joining a club, exercising, reading, and buying anything we can get our hands on are all strategies. Confusing strategies with goals and objectives is not merely a problem in semantics. Rather it suggests that we don't know the difference between what we want (goals and objectives) and how we go about getting what we want (strategies). Too much in our lives is merely an anxious series of strategic moves without consideration of the unstated goals and objectives of these strategies.

Our approach to the formulation of objectives, goals, and strategies is similar to that used in devising our personal philosophy. For example, we might begin with an initial list of twenty-five to thirty objectives and then condense them down to half a dozen or so.

Although it usually makes sense to match up goals with objectives, it is artificial to think of strategies associated with a single objective. Strategies often affect several objectives and goals. How-

Strategic Plan for a Forty-five-year-old Woman

Objectives

1. To establish an identity of my own independent of that of my husband.
2. To help finance the children's college education.
3. To find some form of meaningful employment outside the home.
4. To improve my relationship with my husband and children.
5. To find meaning in my life.

Goals

1. To feel less dependent on my husband financially and emotionally within five years.
2. To earn $25,000 a year from a self-fulfilling job within three years.
3. To decrease the frequency of the power struggles I have with my husband and children to no more than one fight a month.
4. To reduce my level of anxiety about the children and improve my self-esteem significantly by the time I am forty-seven years old.
5. To make it through menopause.

Strategies

1. Seek the occasional advice of a psychotherapist.
2. Take some refresher courses in education and apply for a teaching position.
3. Try to find a suitable religious community with which to affiliate.
4. Enroll in an art and music appreciation program at the local community college.
5. Do some serious reading on philosophy, religion, and psychology.

Strategic Plan for a Twenty-two-year-old Man

Objectives

1. To find meaningful work that enables me to make use of my analytical skills and my people skills for the benefit of society.
2. To have a family.
3. To have sufficient income to support my family.
4. To live in a caring community.
5. To die happy.

Goals

1. To work as a physician's assistant helping poor children in a third world country for three years.
2. To obtain additional training in public health administration by the time I am twenty-six years old.
3. To cultivate my relationship with Kristin with hope that we can be married by the time I am twenty-seven.
4. To have two children before I am thirty-five years old.
5. To have a combined annual family income of $45,000 when I am thirty-five.
6. To avoid hospitalization over the next fifteen years.
7. To enjoy a feeling of closeness and a sense of community with at least fifty people.

Strategies

1. Apply for a position in the Peace Corps or some domestic equivalent and work with poor children for three years.
2. Seek a masters degree in public health administration.
3. Find a job in a rural health clinic located in a small town or village with a strong sense of community.
4. Make time available for my family, my community, and the care and nurturing of my soul.

ever, there should be at least one strategy associated with each objective and goal. To keep our strategic plan manageable, the number of strategies should probably be less than six.

If our ultimate objective is to die happy, as Camus has suggested, then the formulation of a personal strategic plan is an awesome responsibility. For each of us the acid test is, "Are my objectives, goals, and strategies consistent with a happy death?" My strategic plan becomes my plan for crafting my soul. Can I die happy alone on a self-imposed deserted island? Is community a necessary condition for a happy death? Is it possible to die happy, if I live only for today and only for myself?

The example strategic plans of the forty-five-year-old woman and the twenty-two-year-old man are not independent of the plans of their respective "significant others." Couples involved in long-term relationships may want to consider devising a joint strategic plan. Each member of the relationship may begin by preparing his or her own strategic plan independent of the other partner. The tough part of the process involves producing an integrated plan which will satisfy both partners. Not all relationships are strong enough to endure the necessary give-and-take required to negotiate such a joint plan. In some cases, the goals, objectives, and strategies of the respective partners may prove to be so mutually incompatible that an integrated plan is impossible without professional counseling. For better or for worse, such a process forces both partners to put their cards on the table for the other partner to see. A relationship which can survive the stress involved in producing a joint strategic plan may become a more enduring one over the long run.

Two books which many people have found to be particularly useful as preparation for writing their strategic plans are Rollo May's *Freedom and Destiny* and M. Scott Peck's *Road Less Traveled*. May offers sound advice on how to sort out the difference between what we want (our objectives and goals) and the givens in our life (external environment and situation assessment). Reading his book can help us exercise our *freedom* (our choice of objectives, goals, and strategies) to confront our *destiny* (our external environment and our strengths and weaknesses). In Peck's best-selling book, the chapter on discipline provides friendly, low-key guidance on how to make choices in planning one's life.

Above all, what is called for in writing our philosophy and strategy is what Peck calls "dedication to the truth" or personal honesty. Why bother to write a philosophy or a strategy at all, if either is a misrepresentation of the truth? Who are we trying to fool? Ourselves?

Not unlike our personal philosophy, our strategic plan should be subjected to frequent review—at least annually. As our sense of meaning and values evolves and matures, we may want to adjust our strategic plan so that it reflects the changes in who we are and who we want to become. Since the care and nurturing of our soul is a continuous process, our strategic plan should be a living document rather than a one-time effort never to be read again.

Chapter 7

THE LONGING FOR COMMUNITY

What America hungers for is not more goods or greater power, but a manner of life, restoration of the bonds between people that we call community, a philosophy which values the individual rather than his possessions, and a sense of belonging, of shared purpose and enterprise.

RICHARD N. GOODWIN
"THE END OF RECONSTRUCTION" IN
YOU CAN'T EAT MAGNOLIAS

"I'd go stark raving mad in three months," said one student in response to the story of the deserted island. "Life would have no meaning without the possibility of human connectedness." Those who find themselves separated and alone in the midst of hundreds of thousands of others in large cities often find life to be equally unbearable. In the words of Albert Camus, "The thing that lights up the world and makes it bearable is the customary feeling we have of connections with it—and more particularly of what links us to human beings."[1] Life is not a solitary existentialist quest for meaning. It demands a journey outward as well. Nobody is a "self-made" person. We are haunted by an ever-present longing for community—an irresistible need for communication with other human beings, a courageous movement from the "I" to the "we."

Although we are all drawn to the idyllic dream of community, few of us experience real community. What is a community? How do we know whether a particular group is a community or not? *A community is a partnership of free people committed to the care and nurturing of each other's mind, body, heart, and soul through participatory means.* Because we are separated, we can never fully experience another's pain or pleasure. However, through community we can show empathy for another's search for meaning by suspending our own frame of reference so that we may confront the spiritual, intellectual, and emotional world of the other.

The Goal of Human Existence

. . . the goal being a community of free and happy human beings who by constant inward endeavor strive to liberate themselves from the inheritance of anti-social and destructive instincts.

ALBERT EINSTEIN[2]

Opportunities for Community

Although there are endless opportunities for individuals to form communities, few of these alliances result in the establishment of genuine communities which endure very long. Neighborhoods, churches, civic clubs, schools, and fraternal organizations come and go without becoming true communities in which there is real communication or a sense of commitment among members.

The existence of many organizations and groups is a direct response to psychologist Abraham H. Maslow's five hierarchical categories of human needs: (1) physiological requirements (food, water, and shelter), (2) safety (economic security and protection from injury or disease), (3) social acceptance (love, a sense of belonging, and membership in a group), (4) self-esteem (prestige, power, and recognition), and (5) self-actualization (confidence, competence, and achievement).

Interestingly, Maslow places "social acceptance," the need for community, at step 3 in his hierarchy of needs and "self-actualization" at the summit in category 5. Is the actualization of our selves the highest human attainment? We think not. We live in a radically individualized culture, which tends to act as if there is no more important life project than the care and feeding of our detached selves. Yet where is this "self" that is a "self" apart from and without relation to others? Genuine community may be our highest and most difficult human attainment.

In ancient times tribes, clans, troops, and villages existed primarily to protect their members from the ravages of hostile neighbors, wild animals, nature, and starvation. To satisfy our spiritual needs we join churches, synagogues, and other religious organizations. In response to our intellectual and educational needs we attend schools, colleges, and universities. A plethora of groups exists to meet our various needs. But how many of these groups fulfill our deepest longing for community?

At least in principle, it's possible for any group to become a community—a family, a neighborhood, a village, a town, a city, a church, a school, one's workplace, a nation, and maybe even the planet itself. In practice this seldom happens. Why are there so few communities? What is required for a group to evolve into a community? What are the criteria for community?

Criteria for Community

The ultimate test of whether or not a collection of individuals is a community is *whether the members are seriously concerned about one another's well-being.*

Years ago, sociologist Peter Berger spoke of the emergence of "life-style enclaves" in modern America as substitutes for true community as we had once known it. In the life-style enclave, members are drawn together on the basis of a shared interest. There is little struggle to understand another's sense of meaning; rather, life-style enclave members happen to be into some experience or need which periodically assembles them. "The Harley-Davidson Community," "The Airstream Trailer Community," "The Business Community," "The Gay Community," are examples of the way in which "community" has become a designation for a mere "life-style enclave," whose inner life is unworthy of the designation "community." By calling virtually every human gathering a "community," we are saved from the search for true community.

In a church or synagogue, for example, do the members really care about the well-being of one another or is membership in the congregation merely a ticket for improved social status, increased political popularity, or financial gain? Some upscale suburban churches are little more than spiritual annexes of the local country club. They provide a number of services not usually offered by country clubs—weddings, baptisms, and funerals. They offer little in the way of educational programs to deepen the faith of either children or adults. The congregation has almost no connection with the rest of the city—particularly the inner city. Members are uncommitted to anyone other than themselves. The church is thus little more than another means of living in the having mode in a narcissistic culture, a conglomerate of self-consumed individuals.

Shared values and *common aims* also are important characteristics of communities. Although one may enjoy the fellowship of attending the weekly meeting of a civic club, few people are willing to entrust the care and nurturing of their soul to Rotary.

Cooperation, trust, and human empathy are among the shared values which are vital to the formation and survival of communities. But the integration of such values into the life-style of a group may be slow and arduous. Swiss and Austrian alpine villages which embrace these values did not become communities overnight. Rather they have evolved over hundreds of years. We are skeptical of M. Scott Peck's claim in his two books on community, *The Different Drum* and *A World Waiting to Be Born,* that it is possible to lead groups of thirty to sixty persons into community through weekend community-building workshops. We believe that the results of such attempts at instant community-building are more likely to be pseudocommunity—pretend community—rather than enduring community. There are no shortcuts to community. We all say we want community, but do we want to risk the time and energy that community requires?

Real communities are concerned with being—not having. Their members are into sharing, caring, and loving rather than owning, manipulating, controlling, and possessing. Open *communication* and *commitment* to the shared values and common purposes of individual members are of critical importance to the stability of a community. Community survival depends heavily on the ability of members to extend themselves to other members.

A Hasidic Tale

𝒜 prince in a far distant country dreamed of a place where people might live in perfect community—in reciprocal, fair and loving community. The prince called together people to form such a community through a covenant together.

As a sign of their covenant, the prince asked each person to bring a bottle of his or her very finest wine. When they arrived at the place where the covenant was to be made, each person was to take his or her bottle of expensive wine and pour it into a great bowl to symbolize that each person was bringing his or her best gifts to form the community.

A man thought to himself, "If I bring my finest bottle of wine and pour it in with everyone else's wine, what good would that do? All of the distinctive bouquet, flavor, and character of my wine will be lost, swallowed up with everyone else's wine."

He said to himself, "I will take a bottle of my expensive wine, pour out the contents, and fill the bottle with water. Who is to know the difference? That way I will not be wasting my precious vintage."

When the day for the founding of the community came, each person came and poured the content of his or her bottle into the great bowl. Then the prince had everyone take a cup and drink from the bowl. To everyone's horror, all of the wine was water!

Every single person had done what the man had done. They substituted water for wine.

Then the prince knew that he would not have his dream for community. No one there was willing to pay the price for true community.

There is considerable disagreement among social scientists and others as to whether or not *exclusivity* is a prerequisite for community. Should membership in a community be open to all comers or tightly controlled? A village with no entry restrictions soon becomes a town. A town without tough real estate zoning laws grows into a sprawling city. Houston, Texas—the only large city in the United States with no zoning regulations—is an example. Houston—like most cities—represents the antithesis of everything we associate with real communities. In a crazy hodgepodge of residential neighborhoods interspersed with toxic manufacturing plants, noisy thruways, high-rise apartment complexes, and waste-disposal plants, Houston developers have the right to build almost anything almost anywhere. Not inappropriately, the official poster for the 1992 Republican National Convention in Houston featured a rodeo cowboy atop a huge bull with the Houston skyline in the background.

Obviously the severe winter weather and the rugged mountain terrain limit the size of alpine villages. Village size is further constrained by the tough immigration restrictions of Austria and Switzerland. It is not easy for foreigners to purchase a lot in most alpine villages. In a village in the Austrian countryside, nearly everyone is Austrian. On the other hand, exclusive country clubs, which charge $25,000 initiation fees and bar Jews and African Americans from membership hardly qualify as communities.

A certain degree of exclusivity may be necessary during the early stages of development of a community to ensure commitment to shared values and goals. Rapid organizational growth may be incompatible with a stable, enduring community. However, once a community has been firmly established, its members may choose to help nonmembers organize similar communities.

Real communities must also be grounded on a foundation of *equality* and *justice*. However, in no sense are we suggesting that all members of a community must think and act exactly alike. They need not necessarily have the same level of income or wealth. But there cannot be huge disparities among members with regard to the fundamental criteria on which the community is based. In a residential community such as a neighborhood or a village, the community will not flourish if it is dominated by one or two persons who have significantly greater income and wealth than the other members. The same is true of a church or synagogue in which some members are made to feel spiritually or morally inferior to others.

---

*Trouble in the Early Christian
Community with Wealth*

For if a person with gold rings and in fine clothes comes into your assembly, and if a poor person in dirty clothes also comes in, and if you take notice of the one wearing the fine clothes and say, "Have a seat here, please," while to the one who is poor you say, "Stand there," or, "Sit at my feet," have you not made distinctions among yourselves, and become judges with evil thoughts? Listen, my beloved brothers and sisters. Has not God chosen the poor in the world to be rich in faith and to be heirs of the kingdom that he has promised to those who love him? But you have dishonored the poor. Is it not the rich who oppress you? Is it not they who drag you into court? Is it they who blaspheme the excellent name that was invoked over you?

   You do well if you really fulfill the royal law according to the scripture, "You shall love your neighbor as yourself."

James 2:2-8

Empowerment is another important community attribute. The power to influence and shape the direction of the community must be shared equally by all members. Every member is a community leader. This feature of communities may be very threatening to the original founders. For a group to have the possibility of becoming a true community, its organizers must be prepared to risk the complete loss of control over the organization. This is a higher price than most community organizers are prepared to pay. It also gets to the crux of the reason why there are so few communities. *Power sharing is risky business.* Former Soviet Union leader Mikhail S. Gorbachev learned this the hard way, paying the ultimate price for following a six-year strategy of political power-sharing—the collapse and complete disintegration of the Soviet Union. Vaclav Havel, who led Czechoslovakia to freedom in 1989, pursued a very similar strategy, which resulted in the breakup of his country into two independent nations.

   In *A World Waiting to Be Born*, M. Scott Peck expresses the view that it is possible for the CEO of a—large or small—privately owned company to mandate community for the organization. Community cannot be ordered from above. The primary reason that Soviet-style communism failed was that it attempted to impose community on the Soviet people against their will.

Despite all the attention given by American companies to organizational development and employee relations, private businesses not owned by the employees have little chance of becoming communities. The economic and political power gap between the owners and the employees of most companies is not conducive to a sense of community. Top-down community-building initiatives will be perceived by employees as deceptive attempts by management to manipulate them. More often than not, labor-management relations in American companies are so confrontational that they preclude the possibility of community.

Finally, two other noteworthy features of communities are *adaptability* and *conflict resolution*. An enduring community must be able to adapt to a changing external environment in order to survive. Consider the case of public schools in America. Local community support has always been the linchpin of our public schools, but with the complete collapse of any sense of community in most large metropolitan areas, it is hardly surprising to find inner-city schools engaged in a life-or-death struggle. Neither urban neighborhoods nor their schools have been able to keep pace with the rapidly deteriorating socioeconomic conditions found in most cities.

Just as communities must be able to adapt to environmental changes, so too must they be able to resolve their own internal conflicts. Each community needs some sort of conflict resolution mechanism to reduce tensions when disputes arise among individual community members. Obviously, the more open the communication among individual members, the easier it is to resolve conflicts resulting from community pluralism.

The Breakdown of Community

When one tries to find examples of community in today's troubled world, one asks in the words of a popular folk song in the 1960s, "Where have all the flowers gone?" The search for community yields few positive examples and an overwhelming number of places where community has completely broken down—Northern Ireland, the Middle East, Africa, Yugoslavia, Eastern Europe, the former Soviet Union, and the United States to mention only a few. In Northern Ireland the collapse of community involves feuding Protestants and Catholics. In the Middle East are angry Jews and numerous Arab factions; in Africa, there is conflict between tribal leaders and government officials over arbitrary, colonially imposed national boundaries; and in Yugoslavia, the collapse of an ill-conceived marriage of six mutually incompatible republics. As for the rest of Eastern Europe and the former Soviet republics, we have already noted the absence of any spiritual glue to hold them together.

Jesus on Church Conflict Resolution

*I*f another member of the church sins against you, go and point out the fault when the two of you are alone. If the member listens to you, you have regained that one. But if you are not listened to, take one or two others along with you, so that every word may be confirmed by the evidence of two or three witnesses. If the member refuses to listen to them, tell it to the church; and if the offender refuses to listen even to the church, let such a one be to you as a Gentile and a tax collector.

Matthew 18:15-17

Although no war has been fought on American soil since the 1860s, examples of community are not easy to come by. Lamenting the loss of community in the United States, Richard N. Goodwin contends,

> Modern man is confined and often crippled by the world he lives in. A city dweller, he is cut off from sustaining contact with nature. It is almost impossible for the individual to escape the vast and frenzied throng of strangers, stripping him at once of isolation and a place in the community. The dissolution of family and neighborhood and community deprive him of those worlds within a world where he once could find a liberating sense of importance and shared enterprise as well as the security of friends.[3]

Nothing has contributed more to the breakdown of community in America than television and the automobile. One keeps us glued to the privacy of our living room, the other draws us to the road. Neither does much to build community. When we want to go to the bakery, the bank, the grocery store, or our child's school, we hop in the car and drive. There are few places left where neighbors meet—whether it be in the town, the village, or the neighborhood—just to talk, have coffee, and pass the time away. Suburban shopping malls with their pretentious plastic glitter and their moribund parking lots are evidence of our inhumanity and loss of community.

No doubt the nearly two thousand Wal-Mart stores have brought lower retail prices to suburban America as well as small towns scattered throughout the nation. But how many small-town shops and stores have been driven out of business by Wal-Marts? Large discount stores like Kmart and Wal-Mart are no friends of community.

Although there is no shortage of automobiles in Europe, one still finds hundreds of small villages and towns where people actually walk to the local pub, the church, the school, or the market. Many European villages are still connected by railroad passenger trains. Fifty years ago most towns and villages in the United States were linked by passenger trains. Today very few small towns other than in the Northeast have any passenger service whatsoever.

New Town Squares

$\mathcal{M}$alls have become the town squares of our public life, and the brand names and chain stores they host have become the icons of our popular culture.

Washington Post[4]

In the 1940s when one of us was a child visiting his grandfather in a tiny Mississippi village, the most important event each day was the arrival of the Mobile-to-St.-Louis passenger train known as *The Rebel*. *The Rebel* brought the mail, merchandise for Granddaddy's general store, and a handful of passengers—sometimes from faraway places. Black and white farmers alike used to sit on the benches in front of Granddaddy's store dipping snuff, drinking soda waters (soft drinks), and gossiping about who came and went on *The Rebel.*

By trading heavily on the images of their respective small hometowns in the South—Hope, Arkansas, and Carthage, Tennessee—Bill Clinton and Al Gore played to the electorate's longing for community during the 1992 presidential campaign. They promised a return to community but offered few clues as to how this might be achieved.

Why does community elude us? How is it possible for something we claim to cherish so dearly to be found so seldom in the real world? Everybody talks about community, but few are willing to pay the price of forgone narcissism and individualism necessary for community.

Early Christian Community

Now the whole group of those who believed were of one heart and soul, and no one claimed private ownership of any possessions, but everything they owned was held in common. . . . There was not a needy person among them, for as many as owned lands or houses sold them and brought the proceeds of what was sold . . . and it was distributed to each as any had need.

Acts 4:32, 34-35

The very essence of our free enterprise capitalistic system involves promoting the virtues of individualism—often subordinating the interests of the community to those of the individual. The Japanese, on the other hand, take a quite different view of the relationship between the individual and the community. In Japanese companies, for example, the interests of the CEO are subordinated to those of the employees and the customers. The well-being of the group or the community always takes precedence over individual self-interest. Profits are considered to be a reward—bestowed on the company by society for doing a good job—rather than an entitlement. When Boeing, GM, IBM, Sears, and other corporate giants were forced to downsize in the 1990s, they chose to lay off tens of thousands of employees rather than make significant cuts in the salaries of senior executives. So accustomed are most Americans to looking out for number one that they find the loss of control implied by genuine community to be very threatening. Throughout the cold war, community was equated with communism and socialism. Management by committee was frowned on and said to be ineffective and inefficient.

The Lone Ranger

*A*merica and Britain champion individualistic values: the brilliant entrepreneur, Nobel prize winners, large wage differentials, individual responsibility for skills, easy-to-fire-easy-to-quit, profit maximization, hostile mergers and takeovers. Their hero is the Lone Ranger.

LESTER THUROW[5]

Not unrelated to our obsession with individualism is our fondness for authoritarian management. American corporations are among the least democratic institutions in the world. So too is the case with the administration of our universities, nonprofit institutions, and government at all levels. Most Western European companies are much more participatory in their management practices than their American counterparts.

It is not by chance that so few churches and synagogues in America ever evolve into real communities in spite of their spiritual origins. By invoking the authority of God, rabbis, priests, and ministers set themselves apart from the rest of the congregation. In some denominations, local congregations have little or nothing to say about the choice of their priest or minister. A clergyperson is simply assigned to the local congregation by the hierarchy of the denomination.

The Sunday morning service often serves to reinforce the authoritarianism of the minister. The not-so-subtle message is, "I am the conveyor of God's message; therefore, what I have to say should be taken as is." Many parishioners who do not respect military authority—just like Johnny and Sasha—resent the heavy-handed style of autocratic clergy. Others in the congregation willingly turn over their responsibility for community to the pastor. Is it any wonder that so many young people are turned off by organized religion in America? The gap between the congregation and the clergy is so great in most religious congregations that community is illusory.

Unique among Episcopal churches in America in parishioner participation is St. Mark's Church, located on Capitol Hill in Washington, D.C. Each quarter a sermon committee made up entirely of laypersons presents the rector, James R. Adams, with a list of sermon topics for the coming quarter. Two weeks before he delivers a sermon he is given a set of specific questions the committee would like for him to address in the sermon. His homily is presented at the nine o'clock service on Sunday morning, discussed over coffee with parishioners, refined based on their feedback, and then delivered in final form at the eleven o'clock service. This is but one example of many decisions made by parishioners at St. Mark's which are usually made by the clergy in other congregations. St. Mark's parishioners have also devised their own rigorous religious education curriculum, which emphasizes the role of the church in the search for meaning. Not just anyone can teach a Sunday school class at St. Mark's. You must be well trained. Needless to say, there is a very high level of trust between the rector and his parishioners—a level of trust which has evolved over a twenty-five-year period.[6]

Throughout the 1980s, the family and so-called family values received a lot of attention from politicians trying to find issues to arouse the living dead. The family is often cited as an example of community. But is it possible for a family to be a stable community, if there are significant differences in power among the members? In an ideal marriage, the husband and wife may be equal partners. However, from the very moment a child is born and continuing sometimes well into adulthood, it is in an inferior power position relative to its parents. While the child is still very young, its potential to destabilize the family is relatively small. But as it approaches adolescence and begins challenging parental authority, the risk of family instability increases substantially. A family may be a good proving ground for children to learn how to function under a dual command system—a mother and a father—but a community it is not.

The Family Community

I believe that through commitment and hard work it is possible for a family to become a community. Some well-disciplined families use the equivalent of a weekly town meeting to engender trust, draw the family closer together, and build community.

THE PSYCHIATRIST

In the case of the warring factions in the Middle East, Africa, and Eastern Europe, alienation and distrust are obviously large obstacles to peace—not to mention community. The kind of paranoia which existed between the United States and the Soviet Union for more than forty-five years is alive and well in these strife-ridden lands. The cold war ended because Mikhail S. Gorbachev had the courage to break the cycle of distrust and paranoia between the United States and the Soviet Union. Alienation and distrust are antithetical to community whether they be in the family, the city, the church, the workplace, or the nation.

Competing interests among members also can lead to the breakdown of communities. If the real agenda of members is increased personal power and prosperity rather than the well-being of the community, the group will not long remain a community. Sustaining the interest and commitment of members, when they are constantly bombarded by external stimuli provided by politicians, the media, peers, and the like, is a formidable challenge to any community.

Excessive psychological dependency on the group leader or guru also can precipitate the premature death of a community. To launch a new community often requires a charismatic leader. When members become so attached to the leader that they cannot let go—community degenerates into cult of personality. One of the most extreme examples of a cult of personality in recent years was the 1978 mass suicide of 980 followers of California cult leader Jim Jones in Guyana. Jones ordered all of his followers, who had come from America, to commit suicide, and they did. The tragic deaths of more than seventy members of David Koresh's Branch Davidian compound in Waco, Texas, in April 1993 served as a vivid reminder of the risks associated with some cults. Hitler, Mussolini, Stalin, and Mao were destructive cult leaders who operated on a far more grandiose scale than either Jim Jones or David Koresh. They were responsible for the deaths of millions.

Kirkpatrick Sale in his book *Human Scale* has compiled considerable evidence to suggest that sheer size alone is a very important determinant of the long-term viability of a human community. Sale believes there is a size limit beyond which a community should not be allowed to grow if it is to survive. He even goes so far as to propose optimum size limits for what he calls a *neighborhood* and a standard *community*. Sale defines a neighborhood as a group of between 400 and 1,000 people—a face-to-face community such as an Austrian alpine village or a section of a large city. He suggests that 500 people may represent an optimum size for a neighborhood. A community, on the other hand, is an extended group of 5,000 to 10,000 people often consisting of a collection of neighborhoods. A town or a university would fit Sale's definition of a standard community.[7]

If we combine Sale's concern with community size with some of the other formidable obstacles to community just described, then we are led to the inescapable conclusion that it may be virtually impossible for a modern city or nation ever to become a community. Possible exceptions to this rule may include several small European nations—Austria, Finland, Sweden, and Switzerland—which not only enjoy one of the highest standards of living in the world, but also possess some of the attributes of true community.

The Voice of the Earth

*T*he Earth's cry for rescue from the punishing weight of the industrial system we have created is our own cry for scale and quality of life that will free each of us to become the complete person we were born to be.

THEODORE ROSZAK[8]

Notwithstanding the many virtues of community, life in small communities is not without blemishes. Although villages and small towns may be homogeneous and close-knit, they may also be parochial, conservative, resistant to change, and suspicious of outsiders. There is often a low tolerance for nonconformity and opinions that differ from the community norm. Invasion of privacy and nosiness are not uncommon in neighborhoods, villages, and religious congregations. Rarely are envy, greed, and competitiveness absent from small communities. Even though one may live in a community, one may still find oneself detached and estranged from community members. Such experiences may evoke feelings of, "If community life is so great, then why do I feel so bad?"

Some Real Communities

Despite the pessimism we have expressed about the numerous practical obstacles to sustained community, there are examples of genuine community which satisfy most of the criteria just outlined.

Israeli Kibbutzim

The Israeli *kibbutz* movement was started by Eastern European Jews who immigrated to Palestine around the turn of the century hoping to build a Jewish nation. The movement was given increased impetus in 1948 when Israel became an independent state.

A kibbutz is an open-ended agricultural collective of several hundred members in which all property and productive assets are owned by the commune. Membership is open to anyone and no initiation fee is required. Members are free to leave at any time. Land is leased from the Israeli government on a long-term basis. Wages and profits are shared equally by the members, and there are no hired workers from outside the community. The kibbutz builds and furnishes homes for its members, pays for their medical care, provides their food and clothing, and even does their laundry. It also takes care of the elderly.

The kibbutzim have been strongly influenced by the emphasis placed on social justice and community by the biblical prophets. At least initially they were guided by the socialist ideal "from each according to his ability to each according to his needs." Each kibbutz is governed by a general assembly, which meets weekly and is open to all members. The general assembly elects officers and the secretariat, which coordinates the economy. All of the resource allocation decisions are made by the community, including what is to be produced, when it is to be produced, how it is to be produced, and what is to be done with the proceeds.

Twelve Axioms of Community

1. If you don't know where you are going, no road will get you there.
2. If you fear separation, meaninglessness, and death, then unite.
3. The price of community is your own individualism.
4. There is no daddy or mommy, but if there were a daddy or mommy, he or she would be you. (Martin Shubik)
5. Share power—one person, one vote.
6. Might doesn't make right.
7. There's no substitute for commitment and hard work.
8. Small is beautiful.
9. Keep it simple—always make molehills out of mountains.
10. Cooperate and communicate, if you want to survive.
11. Reduce tension; don't escalate conflict.
12. Grow spiritually, intellectually, and emotionally or die.

THE ECONOMIST

For the most part, the highly motivated kibbutzim are more efficient and more productive than other Israeli farms. Today most kibbutzim have diversified economies, which include manufacturing as well as farming. During the thirty-year reign of the Israeli Labor Party, the kibbutzim enjoyed considerable political influence in Israel. Many of the political leaders during that period came from the kibbutzim. Furthermore, some of the settlements in the so-called occupied territories along the borders of Egypt, Jordan, Lebanon, and Syria are kibbutzim.

In spite of the commitment of the kibbutzim to equality and democracy, women are sometimes treated as second-class citizens. Relatively few women are to be found in leadership positions in the kibbutzim. Most of them are employed in domestic services rather than in the more interesting and challenging jobs.

Kirkpatrick Sale has described the kibbutzim as "islands of collectivism in a capitalistic sea. "[9] Although the kibbutzim have managed to avoid most of the social problems found in America, such as alienation, substance abuse, and crime, they have not escaped the negative effects of the ailing Israeli economy caused by the longstanding conflict between the Arabs and the Israelis. The right-wing Likud government of the 1980s was not nearly as supportive of the kibbutzim as had been the case with the Labor Party. The combination of the unstable Israeli political scene and the sagging economy has caused the kibbutzim to back away from some of their socialist ideals. In recent years they have become more pragmatic, less democratic, and more profit-oriented. Kibbutzim can now form joint ventures with outside firms, have outsiders sit on their boards of directors, hire outside workers, and pay workers overtime. Notwithstanding some of these recent changes, the kibbutzim remain one of the purest forms of sustained democratic socialism in history.

Comunidades de Base

Inspired by the Second Vatican Council (1961–65) and Pope Paul VI's 1967 encyclical *Populorum Progressio* (On the Progress of Peoples) but grounded in the widespread poverty and violence in Latin America, a radical form of Christian theology emerged in the 1960s called *liberation theology*. The main thrust of this new theology was a "preferential option for the poor." Within a few years after its inception, liberation theology spawned thousands of small, lay-led Christian communities throughout Latin America. Many of these so-called base communities *(comunidades de base)* literally had their origins in small-village Bible study groups that stressed not Catholic doctrine but community action aimed at solving very real social and economic problems. Some base communities coalesced around very specific projects such as digging a well, building a road, negotiating with wealthy landowners, and defending the village from guerrilla attacks.

Unlike the kibbutzim, collective ownership of the means of production is not a prerequisite for the creation of a base community. Some of the families in the community own their own small plots of land; others do not. However, many villages do own collective farms as well as collective stores, pharmacies, health clinics, and schools. Like the kibbutzim, base communities foster an atmosphere of cooperation, trust, and sharing as well as a strong sense of community.

Consider for example the village of Patzun located near Guatemala City. The Patzun community consists of four hundred families who elect their own officers and governing board. Among the assets owned by the community are a general store, a pharmacy, a school, a small hospital, a children's nutrition program, and an agricultural development center. Through the agricultural development center, the farmers of Patzun have become heavily involved in organic farming. They also produce their own natural fertilizer, herbicides, and insecticides, which are sold in the community's farm supply store. Although most of the families in the village raise vegetables, forty families help support themselves by raising cattle to produce milk, which is sold in the marketplace.

Unfortunately, Latin American base communities have become victims of their own success. Wealthy landowners, conservative Roman Catholics, and right-wing military governments find the community action and direct democracy practiced by base communities to be threatening. Under pressure from Pope John Paul II and the Reagan administration's foreign policy in Latin America, the Catholic Church withdrew its support from base communities in the 1980s and distanced itself from liberation theology. But base communities continue with or without the support of the Catholic Church. In some communities such as Patzun, a modest amount of financial assistance is provided by nongovernment organizations such as the Christian Children's Fund. However, all decisions about how these outside funds are spent are made by the community governing board. So successful was the Patzun community that it was cut loose by the Christian Children's Fund after several years of support.

Although base communities are by no means a panacea, they do offer a mechanism whereby impoverished people can pull themselves up by their bootstraps, so to speak, using a combination of grass-roots democracy and direct action. There may be a great deal that desperate inner-city neighborhoods can learn from base communities. Whether in urban ghettos or Latin American villages, communities can only be formed from within. It is impossible for a national, state, or local government to organize a community by standing outside the group to be organized. Community cannot be mandated by government decree. All the government can do is create incentives, which encourage communities to form, or deterrents, which hasten their demise.

The Church of the Saviour

At least on the surface, The Church of the Saviour in Washington, D.C., also appears to satisfy most of our criteria for community.[10] Started by Gordon Cosby shortly after the end of World War II, The Church of the Saviour is a loose confederation of a dozen or so independent faith communities, each of which is composed of several mission groups. Each community functions as a separate congregation with its own independent leadership, governing council, budget, organization, worship, and membership. However, the faith communities are linked by common parentage and history, deep spiritual ties, continuing fellowship, and interlinking missions.

Common to each community is a deep-seated commitment to a spiritual journey inward as well as an outward journey of service and support for the poor and the oppressed. By virtue of the severe membership requirements of education, worship, prayer, discipline, service, and financial commitment and the belief that the quality of membership is far more important than the number of members, membership in the faith communities rarely exceeds twenty-five.

To become a member of a faith community, one must complete a rigorous two-year education program in five fields: Old Testament, New Testament, Doctrine, Ethics, and Christian Growth. An internship in one of the mission groups also is a membership requirement. Community discipline includes tithing, keeping a personal journal, reporting weekly to the group's spiritual director, fasting, and renewing one's covenant annually.

Membership in a faith community also requires active participation in at least one small mission group. Mission group members are committed to being in continuing relationships with oppressed people. Each mission group has a spiritual director and a moderator. Missions have evolved around such inner-city problems as housing, nutrition, health care, education, and job placement. A relatively new mission is the Joseph's House for homeless men with AIDS.

Three of the faith communities—including The Jubilee Church—hold their weekly worship services in the Potter's House, a coffeehouse and bookstore located in the Adams Morgan section of Washington. The Jubilee Church emerged in response to the need for safe and affordable housing for the poor. The Jubilee Church has been described as "a wild mix of everyone—black and white, rich and poor, the very young and the old, Jew and Gentile, the deeply committed and those who wander in just to eat."[11]

To train faith community leaders and small mission group leaders, The Church of the Saviour operates The Servant Leadership School. The core curriculum of the school consists of five dimensions: (1) servant leadership, (2) community building, (3) spiritual grounding, (4) vocation, and (5) personal response to being with the oppressed.

The faith communities of The Church of the Saviour are based firmly on the Sermon on the Mount ("Blessed are the poor in spirit . . . Blessed are the meek . . . Blessed are they who hunger and thirst for righteousness") and Gordon Cosby's dream of transforming individuals and societies through small groups into communities. If the cycle of poverty is to be broken in our urban areas, it must be attacked at the neighborhood level by small groups; not by sweeping, top-down decrees from Washington, the state capital, or city hall. The small groups attempt to break down the wall which separates the rich and the poor by providing an opportunity for the privileged and the deprived to work together alongside each other. Their aim is to serve the poor "while evoking their gifts and leadership and nourishing genuine friendship."[12]

Leaders of the faith communities of The Church of the Saviour envisage a global network of small, disciplined, self-critical groups and seek empower the poor in our country to connect them with the liberation movement taking place in poor communities throughout the world.

Although many people in the Adams Morgan section of Washington have found new hope for their lives through the faith communities of The Church of the Saviour, there are more and more people falling into despair as poverty, drug abuse, fear, and violence grip not only the neighborhood but the entire city. It is difficult to understand why such a powerful, well-tested approach to community building has not caught on outside a relatively small geographic area. Cynics claim that the limited reach of The Church of the Saviour stems from the pious, self-righteous elitism of its members. Others argue that the price of community demanded by The Church of the Saviour is much higher than most North American Christians are willing to pay.

Alpine Villages

Scattered throughout the Swiss, Northern Italian, Austrian, and Bavarian Alps are hundreds of small villages, practically all of which are several hundred years old. Life in some of these villages comes close to the community ideal we have espoused.

Consider the idyllic Austrian village of Stanzach located in the Lech River valley near Innsbruck. When one gets up in the morning, one does not drive across town to an impersonal shopping mall but rather walks to the village bakery to pick up freshly baked bread and pastries for breakfast. Later in the day one may walk to the grocery store, the bank, the post office, and the farmer's house—in the latter case for milk, butter, and cheese. The village grocery store sells juicy Italian tomatoes—not tasteless plastic ones—and fresh, drug-free chickens. The ice cream is so good that it defies description. Although acid rain has taken its toll in the forests in the Austrian Alps, water pollution is unknown in the Lech valley.

Farming, timber, and tourism are the principal sources of employment in Stanzach. Some people drive thirty miles or so to Reutte, where they work in small factories. As is the case in most alpine villages, there is an inexorable commitment to the land in Stanzach. A gift of land from one's parents carries with it a moral obligation of continued stewardship. Few would think of selling their land and leaving the village.

The church is the center not only of village spiritual life but of social life as well. Friends meet daily at the grocery store, the pub, the inn, the post office, and the churchyard to catch up on village news. Not unlike what is true for most alpine villages, the winters in Stanzach are very severe. But the harshness of winter creates an environment which encourages cooperation, sharing, and trust. The combination of the extraordinary beauty and the severity of the winters provides the glue that holds these communities together. Many alpine villages are linked by an impressive network of passenger trains. Through efficient, high-quality railroads, village residents have easy access to neighboring villages as well as larger cities such as Innsbruck, Munich, Zurich, and Vienna. The railroads provide a sense of connectedness to other parts of the country and to Europe as the case may be.

In these villages, in stark contrast to the rootless mobility that characterizes much of life in America, one finds a sense of continuity where the generations are born, grow up, remain, and eventually die. This type of village mentality pervades all of Switzerland—a country which many consider to be the most democratic and most market-oriented country in the world. Protective agricultural policies in Switzerland and the rest of Western Europe have made it financially feasible for more families to remain in the countryside than is the case in the United States. Conspicuously absent is the dilapidation, deterioration, and decay one finds throughout the American rural South.

Over the past 700 years, Switzerland has devised a unique social and political structure with a strong emphasis on federalism and direct democracy, which brings together in its twenty-six cantons (tiny states) four languages and cultures—German (spoken by 65 percent of the population), French (18 percent), Italian (10 percent), and Romansh (1 percent). The cantons and 3,020 communes enjoy considerable autonomy. Several cantons still follow the centuries-old tradition of the *Landsgemeinde* or open-air parliaments each spring. Although Swiss women have been allowed to vote in federal elections since 1971, several cantons and communes still do not permit women to vote in local elections.

Switzerland has a coalition governnment with a rotating presidency in which the president serves for a period of only one year. Not surprisingly, many Swiss do not know the name of their own president.

A petition signed by 100,000 voters can force a nationwide vote on a proposed constitutional change. The signatures of only 50,000 voters can force a national referendum on any federal law passed by parliament.

In Switzerland, the primary responsibility for social welfare rests with the cantons and the communes. Unlike the United States, where 37 million Americans have no health insurance whatsoever and another 50 million are underinsured, 95 percent of all Swiss citizens are insured against illness by one of the four hundred *private* health insurance funds.

At an early age, Swiss children are taught in public schools the virtures of self-sufficiency, hard work, cooperation, and loyalty to family and community. Since public assistance is funded from local sources, it behooves the local community to discourage public dependency and to work with social welfare clients so that they become self-sufficient as soon as possible. Public welfare is viewed as temporary—lasting only so long as the victim is impoverished.

Aid plans are custom-designed on an individual basis with strict time limits imposed. The contract between the client and the local welfare agency is approached from a win-win perspective in which the objective is to help the client get back on his or her feet. For the sum of five francs, it is possible to obtain any individual's tax return without having to state a reason. This helps keep not only welfare clients honest but others as well.

The Swiss actually practice what many politically conservative Americans preach but rarely practice themselves—complete decentralization of the responsibility for social welfare. The incidences of poverty, homelessness, drug abuse, violence, and crime are significantly lower in Switzerland than in the United States. Unfortunately, Zurich with Europe's biggest drug abuse and AIDS problem, has become an ignoble exception to the Swiss rule. Before it was closed by the police, the once-elegant Platzpitz Park had become an open market for drugs and drug-related paraphernalia.

Even with its many virtues, Switzerland is not without some severe critics. Some view Switzerland as an arrogant, racist, sexist, xenophobic nation whose citizens are concerned only about themselves.

In spite of their fierce independence, Swiss towns, villages, and cantons do cooperate on important projects involving the general public interest, including railroads, highways, tunnels, electric energy, water supply, and pollution abatement. The inescapable conclusion engendered by a visit to Switzerland is that Switzerland not only works, but it works very well. It works because Switzerland is a tiny, hard-working, very democratic country with a strong sense of community. What can a global superpower like the United States learn from a small country with only 6.6 million people? A lot.

The Politics of Meaning

The politics of meaning represents a paradigm switch from a discourse of materialism and selfishness to a discourse of caring and community. The psychological, ethical, and spiritual needs, though not reducible to something quantifiable or easily subject to scientific observation, are validated as equally important with material needs and quantifiable data.

A politics of meaning aims to encourage collective action to shift these societal priorities and to restructure economic and political institutions. It also seeks to encourage a shift in the dominant discourse, so that ethical, psychological, and spiritual needs are no longer seen as "soft" or irrelevant, but rather as fundamental to what it is to be a human being.

MICHAEL LERNER
Tikkun, July/August 1993

Some Hopeful Signs

Notwithstanding the many obstacles to community and the infrequency of its occurrence in the real world, there are several encouraging signs suggesting increased receptivity to such ideas both in the United States and elsewhere. For example, the two widely read books, *Habits of the Heart* and *The Good Society,* by Robert N. Bellah and his colleagues, are a clarion call for community. Although neither of these books is long on solutions, they do define very clearly the problems of excessive individualism and lack of community in America.

Eight Steps to Community

1. *Shared Values*—identify shared values and community objectives.
2. *Boundaries*—define the community's boundaries.
3. *Empowerment*—create a system of governance and a community decision-making process that empowers all community members.
4. *Responsibility Sharing*—implement a community-wide responsibility-sharing system.
5. *Growth and Development*—formulate and implement strategies for spiritual, intellectual, and emotional growth and development as well as physiological well-being.
6. *Tension Reduction*—devise a conflict resolution mechanism to reduce tension among community members and between the community and those living outside community boundaries.
7. *Education*—provide members with education and training on community values, decision making, governance, responsibility, growth and development, and tension reduction.
8. *Feedback*—implement an adaptive feedback control system which monitors community performance against objectives and adjusts community strategies accordingly.

THE ECONOMIST

A small group of economists led by Amitai Etzioni has become increasingly disillusioned with its profession's role as the defender of narcissism, hedonism, and greed and has proposed an alternative paradigm to the neoclassical model of economics, in which community values such as sharing, caring, and cooperating take priority over egoism, individualism, and materialism. This new approach to economics, known as the *communitarian movement,* advocates balancing the efficiency and productivity benefits of a market-driven economy against the offsetting environmental, social, and human costs. These economists are not opposed to the use of markets to allocate resources, but rather feel that community values are often given short shrift by unrestrained capitalism. The so-called third world base communities already described are good examples of communitarian economics. Not only is it important how resources are allocated by the economy, but it is also important how people participate in this process. Etzioni's book *The Spirit of Community* is a timely response to a heartfelt social need.

We have had a lot to say about the alienation, despair, and lack of community among minorities, the poor, and the homeless living in our inner cities. But many people who fled the problems of the city and took refuge in the suburbs have found that life in the suburbs is not quite what it was cracked up to be. Not only have crime and drugs followed them to the suburbs, but they find themselves isolated and separated from their neighbors in their air-conditioned, burglarproof, split-level homes enclosed by protective fences.

When one of us was asked by the minister of an upscale suburban church what could be done about the lack of community in the area near his church, it was tempting to answer cynically, "The people are here by choice. They rejected the old neighborhoods in the city where there once was a sense of community." But upon further reflection, it was realized that this minister was expressing the genuine pain and anguish of his congregation. It is not possible to solve a problem if you don't even know the problem exists. People living in the suburbs are becoming increasingly aware that they too have a problem called meaninglessness and that all of the shopping malls, computer-controlled burglar alarms, and private police forces in the world are not going to provide them with meaning or make them feel any less lonely. They need community, and they know it.

Even though the number of farms in the United States decreased by 50 percent to just over two million during the past three decades, the number of small farms has once again started to increase in the 1990s. Highly educated, part-time farmers who farm for pleasure, profit, and the quality of life which farming brings have begun sprouting their crops on the fringes of cities all over the United States. These sophisticated weekend farmers grow organic herbs, exotic lettuces, snow peas, and miniature vegetables. Although it's too soon to label this development a "return to the countryside" movement, it is nevertheless an encouraging sign.

According to the Fellowship of Intentional Community (FIC), today there are more people seeking community and more groups starting new ones than at any time since the late 1960s. There are more than 3,000 intentional communities in the United States, 350 of which are described in the *Directory of Intentional Communities* published by the FIC. As defined by the FIC,

> An *intentional community* is a group of people living cooperatively, dedicated by intent and commitment to specific communal values and goals, with group members in continual, active fellowship around these mutual interests. Fellowship life is facilitated inside each community by a uniquely defined governing body which uses established, though sometimes diverse, decision-making processes. Generally, intentional communities place high value on the shared ownership or lease of a common home place—housing, land, businesses—which often serve to demonstrate communal values and goals to the wider society.

Many communities are reporting the highest population numbers in more than a decade. Some are completely full, and others have long waiting lists.

These intentional communities range in size and emphasis from small agricultural homesteads with only a few families to villagelike communities similar to the Israeli kibbutzim consisting of several hundred members. One of the best-known intentional communities is Twin Oaks. Founded in 1967, Twin Oaks is an agricultural commune situated on 460 acres of woods, hilly pasture, and wood-land near Charlottesville, Virginia. Its eighty-five members support themselves by manufacturing handcrafted hammocks and produc-ing various agricultural products such as milk, cheese, soy foods, tofu, and vegetables. Twin Oaks uses a planner-manager system of government adopted from B. F. Skinner's novel, *Walden Two*.

Koinonia Partners is a simple life-style, Christian community located in Americus, Georgia, which was established in 1942. Its ministries include home construction for low-income families, child develop-ment, and peace witness. Income is earned from farming as well as the community's pecan, fruitcake, and candy mail-order business.

Another place where community thrives is in the tiny state of Vermont. With a population of only half a million people, Vermont seems to share a number of common values with Switzerland—in-dependence, democracy, hard work, and a strong sense of commu-nity. Influenced by some of its earlier Iroquois and Yankee inhabitants, Vermont is one of the few remaining places in America where "the hills are still alive with the sound of town and village, of neighborhood, corner, and place."[13] Vermont is small enough to be politically manageable. The key to Vermont's strong democratic tradition is the state's 246 town governments in which the chief executive officer is a three-member or five-member board and the legislative arm is the legendary town meeting. In 1990, Vermont voters sent an independent socialist to Congress—the first socialist to be elected to Congress in half a century. Although Vermont is too small to save the nation, it does provide an example of an alternative life-style and quality of life seldom found today in the United States.

The Role of Community in the Search

Not unlike the search for meaning, community building is slow and arduous. Few have succeeded at it, but the potential rewards are substantial. Community is about cooperation, sharing, commit-ment, trust, justice, empowerment, adaptability, and tension reduc-tion—values acclaimed by many but achieved by few.

The reason community is so important to those of us involved in the quest for meaning stems from the specter of separation, meaninglessness, and death. We know that we are separated from ourselves, others, and the ground of our being. We are also haunted by the deep and lingering fear that our life may have no meaning at all. As if separation and meaninglessness were not enough for our soul to endure, we must also deal with the uncertainty and apparent nothingness of our own death.

A community is a continuing, laboratory test-site for life, love, meaning, soul crafting, and death. In community, we receive encouragement and guidance from others for our search. It can also be a source of fun, fellowship, humor, and great joy for the young and the old, the well-to-do and the not-so-well-to-do, the educated and the uneducated.

We believe that community not only can reduce our separateness, but it can also facilitate our search for meaning and help us come to terms with our finiteness. Through community we can close some of the gaps which separate us and work together to seek meaning confronting our common plight, namely death. Community is one of the most important openings to our soul—a window of opportunity for a happy death.

Chapter 8

THE SEARCH FOR MEANING IN THE WORKPLACE

Neither possession, nor power, nor sensuous satisfaction, . . . can fulfill man's desire for meaning in his life; he remains in all this separate from the whole, hence unhappy. Only in being productively active can man make sense of his life.

ERICH FROMM
MARX'S CONCEPT OF MAN

The Meaning of Work

For some artists, writers, musicians, physicians, and clergy, the meaning of life lies entirely in their work—in their creations, in their patients, and in their congregation. Many corporate executives, politicians, and government officials seek meaning through manipulation, power, and control. Still others work only because it enables them to accumulate vast wealth and material possessions. But for millions of people, work is a necessary evil engaged in primarily to support themselves and their families. For them, work is not a source of pleasure but rather a boring, repetitive, and unchallenging way of making a living. About work Albert Camus once said, "What sordid misery there is in the condition of a man who works and in a civilization based on men who work."[1] The number of people who enjoy their work and find it truly meaningful are a minority of the population.

The love affair most Americans have with their weekends provides further evidence of the alienation which exists in the American workplace. Is the weekend a clever Madison Avenue marketing ploy to increase consumer spending? Or is it a soothing balm to assuage the alienation and meaninglessness of the workplace?

In the United States, 77.4 percent of the workers work for business, 15.2 percent for government, and 7 percent for themselves. What determines whether or not one's work is meaningful? Does it depend entirely on the job itself? Are some jobs inherently more meaningful than others? What role does the employer play in influencing the meaningfulness of a particular job? What about the attitude of the employee? How does one go about finding meaningful work? These questions will be addressed in this chapter.

Meaninglessness in the Workplace

Since more than three-fourths of the work force in the United States is employed by business, we shall devote special attention to the problem of meaninglessness in the business world. As we noted in the story of Johnny and Sasha, American companies are among the least democratic institutions in the world. In most companies—large or small—only a handful of people have any significant influence over the answers to such fundamental strategic questions as:

1. In which businesses should we be?
2. What should be our level of commitment to each business?
3. How should we finance our businesses?
4. In which countries should we operate?
5. How should we organize?
6. What should we research and develop?
7. What should we produce?
8. How should we produce?
9. To whom should we sell?
10. How should we sell?

The typical employee has little input into decisions related to such matters as hiring and firing, salaries and wages, fringe benefits, working conditions, mergers, acquisitions, divestitures, and plant closings.

But today's blue-collar and white-collar workers alike are well educated and affluent and have little respect for top-down authoritarian management. They resent being told what to do by anyone. This incongruity between modern employees and the business environment goes a long way toward explaining the increase in absenteeism among industrial employees, declining productivity, and America's weakened competitive position abroad. Undemocratic, hierarchical organizations make community building in the workplace impossible and discourage the search for meaning. The huge salary gap between the CEO and employees in most companies does little to engender confidence, trust, and community.

According to the Bureau of Labor Statistics, 20 percent of the college graduates in the 1980s accepted jobs that did not require college degrees. These jobs were often low-wage, dead-end positions with stagnating or declining real incomes associated with them. For many corporate jobs which require a college degree, the importance of the degree to job performance is often minimal. A surprisingly large number of employees and managers are significantly over-educated for their boring, mindless jobs. One of the reasons that downsizing corporate staffs meets with so little resistance in the United States is that many of the managers who are let go are woefully underemployed.

Another factor contributing to the sense of meaninglessness and powerlessness in the workplace is the confrontational nature of labor-management relations in America. The history of the American labor movement is a story of mutually destructive labor-management conflict. The American approach to industrial relations has always been based on a macho zero-sum mind-set, in which management perceived that labor's gains would result in equivalent losses for management. Organized labor's view has been much the same—labor's gains can be achieved only by imposing comparable costs on management.

Since the end of World War II, the Congress and state legislatures have passed a plethora of statutes aimed at curbing the power of labor unions and making it either illegal or extremely difficult to carry out a successful labor action against an employer. Most states have laws which ban strikes against state and local governments, and it is illegal for federal employees to go out on strike against the U.S. Government. While our government vigorously supported the establishment of so-called free labor unions in Eastern Europe, it was simultaneously doing everything possible to destroy free labor unions in the United States.

No American president has ever been more effective in under-mining the economic and political power of organized labor than Ronald Reagan. In 1981, when he fired 11,500 striking air traffic controllers and broke the back of PATCO, the air traffic control-lers' union, President Reagan sent a clear signal to corporate executives that not only was union busting condoned, but it was in fact official government policy. Company after company re-sponded with strike-breaking and wage and benefits roll-back strategies of their own.

During the Reagan years the courts consistently allowed corpo-rations to dismiss striking workers—sometimes with twenty-five to thirty years seniority—and hire permanent replacements. Food stamps for striking workers were cut off in some areas. The National Guard and highway patrol were called in by state governors to protect management, escort strike-breakers, and harass strikers. Unions have often isolated themselves from local communities and unorganized workers, and have been unable to throw off the "special interest" jacket so effectively "custom-tailored" for them by Corporate America.

Through the use of strike-breakers and the heavy-handed tactics of the Virginia highway patrol, the Pittston Coal Group brought 1,900 striking United Mine workers to their knees in Virginia, West Virginia, and Kentucky in 1989. Hostile court actions and the antiunion tactics of Virginia Governor Gerald L. Baliles proved to be very costly for the beleaguered Pittston miners. The Pittston strike was a typical American industrial relations action. Both sides managed to inflict enormous pain on the opposing party. When the strike was finally settled nine months later, the badly battered union received only marginal, face-saving concessions from Pittston. Although labor and management claimed publicly that the settlement contract reflected a "win-win" situation, there were no winners in the Pittston strike.

Contrary to what we were promised by business leaders, the decline in the American labor movement has not resulted in a corresponding increase in productivity. Blue-collar workers are more alienated than ever. American companies now face even more intense competition from Japan, Pacific Rim nations, and the European Community.

Who is to blame for the confrontational labor-management relations, which have persisted in this country throughout the twentieth century? There is plenty of blame to share on both sides.

Labor-management relations in Europe are much more participatory and less confrontational than in the United States, reflecting a combination of enlightened corporate and union leadership as well as extensive legislation protecting the rights of employees.

Although unions in Europe are much stronger than they are in the United States, there are far fewer strikes or severe labor conflicts than in the United States. Unions in western Germany, Sweden, Finland, and Austria are very powerful but have leaders who know a great deal about what's going on in the industries they represent. Unlike those in the United States, European labor laws are heavily biased in favor of employees rather than management. It is, for example, very difficult to fire an employee for any reason other than a demonstrable decline in business. Employees have strong legal protection from indiscriminate layoffs.

Labor-management relations in Europe are based more on a spirit of cooperation rather than conflict. Both corporate managers and labor leaders know the limits of their power and understand that, if the enterprise cannot successfully compete in the international marketplace, then both sides will lose. There is more of a win-win attitude rather than the divisive zero-sum approach, which characterizes American labor-management relations.

We do not mean to imply that employee relations in all American companies are based on distrust and confrontation. IBM, Federal Express, Delta Air Lines, United Parcel, and Burroughs Wellcome are just a few of the many companies in the United States which do approach their employees in an enlightened, nonconfrontational fashion. For many years IBM and Delta had no layoff policies, guaranteeing the jobs of their employees during economic downswings. Unfortunately, competitive pressures in the 1990s forced both companies to back away from their full-employment policies.

Although it is not the responsibility of a business to provide meaning to the lives of its employees, the business will pay a high price if its employees cannot find meaning either within the company or in their private lives. Undemocratic, hierarchically organized companies with a confrontational management style are not conducive to the search for meaning in the workplace.

Alienation

As we have said, alienation stems from separation from oneself, from others, and from one's grounding. Alienation in the workplace is the result of an individual's being transformed into a dehumanized thing or object through work itself.

According to one pessimistic view, the only way to avoid alienation in the workplace is to be self-employed. Karl Marx said, "A being does not regard himself as independent unless he is his own master, and he is only his own master when he owes his existence to himself. A man who lives by the favor of another considers himself a dependent being."[2] Or in the cogent words of Albert Camus, "There is dignity in work only when it is freely accepted."[3]

In our highly organized, mass-production, consumer-driven, capitalistic society, many dream of the possibility of being self-employed. Few succeed at it. Since self-employment is not a feasible option for most Americans, we shall examine some of the problems of alienation and meaninglessness among those employed in business, agriculture, education, health care, and government.

If one chooses to pursue a career in business, is it possible to have a meaningful career regardless of the nature of the business? Does it matter whether the business is textiles, tobacco, pharmaceuticals, chemicals, plastics, nuclear weapons, or disposable diapers? Are there any differences in the degree of meaningfulness associated with different jobs such as accounting, finance, marketing, production, research and development, and personnel? What about the objectives of the business? Are profit maximization, service, quality, full employment, and good citizenship equally meaningful business objectives?

These are not easy questions. Their answers depend on our personal philosophy—our sense of meaning, our values, our ethical principles, and our sense of social responsibility. For example, if one considers killing a human being to be an act of nihilism, how is it possible to go to work either for a defense contractor or for a cigarette manufacturer? If one is opposed to the exploitation of the indigenous people of Central America, how can one support either explicitly or implicitly the policies of American companies that contribute to the oppression of these people? Is the design of manipulative television advertisements aimed at Saturday morning cartoon viewers a legitimate vocation for those who derive meaning from children?

Today there are few products manufactured in America for which there are not at least some adverse social consequences, ranging from carcinoma and toxicity to wounds from unsafe appliances, toys, and automobiles. Finding employment in a business consistent with one's sense of meaning can be a difficult challenge. All too many people are seduced into meaningless jobs by the promise of high salaries and liberal perquisites. The implicit contract offered by many companies is, "In return for your soul, we promise you fame, fortune, and power."

With its avowed policy of "caring capitalism," Ben & Jerry's, the Vermont ice cream maker, stands at the forefront of enlightened, socially responsible American businesses. No senior executive at Ben & Jerry's earns more than seven times the compensation of the lowest-paid worker with at least one year at the company. Its "partnershops" located in low-income areas are joint ventures with nonprofit, community-minded organizations aimed at creating employment opportunities, helping revitalize poor neighborhoods, and empowering neighborhood residents. In 1991, when dairy prices plummeted, Ben & Jerry's paid Vermont farmers premium prices for dairy products, reflecting what the company called its determination to support family farmers. Ben & Jerry's has one of the most liberal employee benefit programs in the United States.

Ben & Jerry's Employee Benefits

1. a pension program with company matching funds of up to 2 percent of an employee's salary
2. medical and dental insurance (company paid)
3. group term life insurance
4. disability insurance
5. adoption support (The company will pay for the cost of an adoption.)
6. maternity, paternity, and adoption leave (paid leave without loss of job rights and benefits)
7. health clubs (free memberships in several area health clubs)
8. confidential employee counseling (company paid)
9. cholesterol screenings, hearing exams, and other wellness services (periodic)
10. massage therapy (periodic)
11. profit-sharing
12. guarantees on bank loans for house downpayments
13. employee stock purchase (15 percent below market price)
14. tuition aid
15. childcare (on-site with sliding fee schedule)
16. three free pints of ice cream a day (factory seconds)
17. fresh-baked, free chocolate cookies delivered to everyone on Fridays

---

While the sixty-year exodus of small farmers to American cities continues, the family farm remains a cherished tradition in Western Europe. The European Community supports ten times the number of farmers found in our country. Unlike their counterparts in the United States, small farms are still considered to be a valued way of life in Europe. Reflecting the low priority Americans place on the family farm, traditional farming has been devoured and replaced by huge, corporate-owned megafarms. More than half the food in America is now produced by only 4 percent of our farms. Corporate farms are increasingly dependent on chemicals, pesticides, and energy-guzzling methods of raising crops and transporting them long distances to market. Corporate farmers are obsessed with high crop yields, which destroy rather than nurture the soil. As family farms fade away, so too do rural communities including businesses, schools, and hospitals.

African Americans in particular were not motivated to remain on the exploitative tenant farms to which they were relegated after the Civil War. Anything Chicago, Cleveland, or Detroit had to offer was better than life in the Mississippi Delta. The quality of education, medical care, cultural life, transportation, and public utilities available throughout rural America in the 1940s and 1950s provided little incentive for white farmers to remain in the countryside either. There was an arrogant attitude among our increasingly urban population that life on the farm was not worth preserving.

We have paid dearly for our myopic views and policies toward rural America. Many of our worst urban social and economic problems are directly attributable to our inability to create a more balanced approach to urban and rural development since World War II.

Back to the Farm

*A*griculture should once again be in the hands of the farmers—people who own the land, the meadows, the orchards, and the livestock, and take care of them. In part these will be small farmers who have been given back what was taken from them, in part larger family farms, and in part modest cooperatives of owners or commercial enterprises. The farmers themselves know best—and new farmers will quickly learn—how to renew the ecological balance, how to cultivate the soil and gradually bring it back to health. I also believe that a portion of the agricultural land should simply be left fallow, converted to pastureland, or reforested.

VACLAV HAVEL
Summer Meditations

Unlike the case in the United States, agricultural subsidies in Europe have been designed to protect small farmers. While it is true that European farms are much smaller and less efficient than

---

Family Farming

We believe the survival of the family farm is vital—and not just to us as a business making ice cream from 4 million gallons of fresh Vermont milk and cream every year. Family farming is crucial to all of us. It's the historic, living foundation of our food supply, our values, and the rural communities from which our country has always drawn strength, character and economic security.

BEN & JERRY'S

American farms and food costs are higher, there are many compensating benefits. Since small European farms use fewer nitrates, pesticides, and herbicides, wells and streams are much less likely to be contaminated than in the United States. Because the quality of life has remained high in small European towns and villages, one does not find the urban poverty, crime, homelessness, and despair in European cities that one finds in New York, Washington, Los Angeles, and Detroit.

What we have managed to do in this country over the past half a century is transfer the alienation, poverty, and despair of the small family farmer from the countryside to the inner-city ghettos of our large metropolitan areas—a subject which is rarely mentioned in political campaigns. Meaninglessness is not a topic with which our politicians feel very comfortable.

Unfortunately the problem of alienation is not limited to those who work in business or on the farm. That colleges and universities are so ineffective in helping their students find meaning in their lives should come as no surprise. Excessive academic professionalism, research grantsmanship, and functional isolationism are evidence of the disarray and absence of community on college campuses. Professors are engaged in an intense competition for promotions, research grants, and their share of a decreasing pool of funds for faculty salary increases.

There is little evidence to suggest that our colleges and universities possess either the will or the leadership to lead our nation out of the "me" generation of the 1980s. They are an integral part of the problem rather than a catalyst for change. Academic politics appears to be far more important to many faculty members than the care and nurturing of their students.

Fifty years ago a physician was a devoted public servant who called on his patients in their homes, would accept payment in kind (a chicken, a sack of tomatoes, or a fifth of whiskey), and frequently was not paid at all. Today the entire health care system in America is driven by greed and our intense fear of death. Physicians, private profit-making hospitals, and health insurance companies are engaged in a never-ending struggle to extract as much money as possible from patients, employers, and the government. How can a physician work for a for-profit hospital and still be bound by loyalty to the patient? The title of the lead article in a medical practice marketing journal said it all—"How to Build a $1 Million Practice in 24 Months." So intense was the economic pressure to fill the beds in some private psychiatric hospitals in the 1980s, that perfectly normal people with good health insurance were committed against their will to these highly profitable hospitals for one and only one reason—their insurance money. Hospitals now advertise on TV—"Come have your cancer surgery with us!"

Presidents Jimmy Carter, Ronald Reagan, and George Bush were each elected by running against the federal government in Washington. The picture they painted of our civil servants was one of a bunch of incompetent, lazy bureaucrats who drain the coffers of the public and create nothing of value for society. After sixteen years of such shabby treatment by their CEOs, it is hardly surprising to find the self-esteem of many full-time government officials at an all-time low. When Senator Tim Wirth—one of many congressmen and senators who chose not to seek re-election in 1992—decided to leave the Senate, he said, "Politics has made me a person I don't like."

A nation which holds its government in such utter contempt cannot expect its politicians and professional government employees to be paragons of honesty, creativity, and efficiency. So long as the "we versus them" mentality persists, our government will remain bogged down in a quagmire of meaninglessness. As Richard Goodwin has observed, "Asking many of today's institutions to respond to new needs is a little like putting a man on a windowsill and asking him to fly. Not only was he not built for flight but if you keep insisting he's likely to turn around and punch you in the nose."[4]

Meaningful Government

The liberty of this country and its great interests will never be secure if its public men become mere menials to do the biddings of their constituents instead of being representative in the true sense of the word, looking to the lasting prosperity and future interests of the whole country.

LUCIUS QUINTUS CINCINNATUS LAMAR
Southern Statesman

Management Philosophy

What seems to be missing in many American companies is a well-defined sense of direction for senior management that goes beyond narrowly defined financial targets. Are there reasons other than simply maximizing shareholders' wealth as to why an enterprise should exist in the first place? Is it important to communicate senior management's sense of purpose, values, and ethical principles to employees, customers, suppliers, shareholders, and the public? An increasing number of successful companies such as Burroughs Wellcome, Ben & Jerry's, Johnson and Johnson, and United Parcel Service seem to think the answer to this question is, yes. These companies have all devised formal statements of management philosophy.

A philosophy of management is concerned with the fundamental principles on which the affairs of a business are based. It should capture the sense of meaning and direction of the senior management. A well-thought-out management philosophy will have significant impact on the company's goals, objectives, strategies, and policies as well as the corporate culture and style of management. Not unlike a personal philosophy, a management philosophy is a mirror image of the heart and soul of senior management. It defines the core of management's existence. It should provide a clear signal to employees as to what the business is all about.

The rationale underlying the need for a management philosophy was succinctly captured by Tennessee Williams in his play *The Glass Menagerie:* "Man is by instinct a lover, a hunter, a fighter and none of these instincts are given much play at the warehouse." Because these instincts have been given so little attention by corporate strategists, it is not surprising to find a number of corporate giants floundering aimlessly in a sea of economic chaos. Corporations whose leaders have no clearly defined sense of meaning or direction in their personal lives have great difficulty motivating employees to climb on board a leaderless ship.

Machismo

If you're not a risk-taker, you should get the hell out of business.

STEVEN J. ROSS
Time Warner

Every company—large or small—has a management philosophy. In most cases it has never been formally expressed and written down on a sheet of paper for circulation to the employees. Instead, it exists only in the head of the company's CEO. Few companies have taken the time or effort required to compose a formal management philosophy.

There are several reasons why it may be beneficial for senior management to devise a formal statement of philosophy. Very often when management attempts to reach a consensus over the company's philosophy, it turns out that different managers have radically different understandings of the company's fundamental principles. When there is no written statement spelling out management's basic principles, honest differences of opinion may go unnoticed for a long time; and they may be difficult to resolve when they do come to light. Furthermore, the limitations of unwritten communications become more obvious the larger the company becomes.

Later-generation employees who have never met the founder may have only a distorted view of the founder's original vision of the company. The older a company becomes and the more removed it is from the founder, the more important it is to have a written version of the company's philosophy.

The absence of a well-defined management philosophy implies a certain lack of discipline on the part of top management, a lack of commitment to a specific set of principles. This lack of commitment soon becomes obvious to all the company's other managers and employees. Such a company is easily jerked around by its external environment including competitors, customers, and politicians.

A meaningful management philosophy should address the questions: What does the company do *for people?* What does it do *to people?* How do *people participate* in the business activities of the company? Not surprisingly, the elements of a management philosophy are very similar to those of a personal philosophy: (1) a sense of meaning, (2) a statement of values, (3) ethical principles, and (4) a statement of corporate responsibility.

Surely the most difficult step for a manager in formulating a management philosophy involves expressing his or her sense of meaning. Very few managers are comfortable in sharing their views on the meaning of life with their colleagues. Often one has to resort to indirect means to encourage managers to articulate their feelings on what life means to them.

No matter how elusive the search for meaning may be, it behooves senior management to give considerable thought to how it can create an environment that encourages managers and employees alike to find meaning in their individual lives. There are no quick and easy answers to questions related to life's meaning, but corporations should be aware of and recognize the importance of this subject to the mental health of their employees. Although corporations are not in the meaning business, it is an act of irresponsibility for a corporation to stifle its employees' quest for meaning.

Once management has expressed its sense of meaning, it may then consider the question of basic managerial values. Given the amount of discipline required to formulate a statement of values, it is frequently necessary to employ an outside facilitator to help senior management articulate its values. Psychologists, theologians, and philosophers have been used as effective catalysts to the process of value formulation. Obviously, arriving at a consensus on corporate values may take considerable effort if the management group is relatively heterogeneous with respect to values. Indeed, there is the risk of creating a rift among managers if serious value differences come to the surface.

Burroughs Wellcome's Values

1. Integrity
2. Ethics
3. Respect for the Individual
4. Teamwork
5. Commitment for Research

6. Innovation
7. Quality
8. Citizenship
9. Efficiency
10. Adaptability

Until very recently, IBM was considered one of the best-managed multinational companies in the world. It built its well-deserved reputation on three basic beliefs—respect for the individual, customer service, and excellence. Whether one was visiting an IBM office in Munich, Chicago, Helsinki, or Rio de Janeiro, there was a consistency about IBM throughout the world. One knew what to expect from IBM everywhere. And as we have noted, an integral part of IBM's consistency and high level of performance was its full-employment policy. However, in the 1990s a new value rose to the top of the IBM priority list—*efficiency*. A once great company now finds itself reeling in its unsuccessful attempts to defend itself from leaner, meaner competition through a strategy based on *restructuring* and *downsizing*.

If a company's management philosophy contains too many values, then they may not be taken seriously by the employees. Management may be perceived by some as trying to be all things to all people. It is better to go with a shorter list of values in which you truly believe, than to misrepresent the values of management.

A number of well-known companies including American Airlines, Bristol-Myers, Data General, Eli Lilly, and IBM have attempted to express their ethical principles and communicate them to their employees through a code of ethics. These codes of ethics vary in length from one-page summaries of several ethical principles to lengthy, detailed treatments of corporate policies covering many different aspects of corporate life.

IBM's thirty-page *Business Conduct Guidelines* is by far the most elaborate example of a corporate code of ethics. It covers a broad range of topics ranging from protecting IBM's assets to fairness to competitors, bribery, gifts, business entertainment, conflict of interest, and anti-trust laws. For employees confronted with some ethical dilemma, IBM offers the following advice:

> Ask yourself: If the full glare of examination by associates, friends, even family were to focus on your decision, would you remain comfortable with it? If you think you would, it probably is the right decision.[5]

Each employee has a copy of this document and on an annual basis must sign a statement indicating familiarity and compliance with its contents. Notwithstanding the company's recent problems, the IBM *Business Conduct Guidelines* has become a widely emulated model.

Given a set of values and ethical principles, how does one go about applying them to the various stakeholders of the company— investors, employees, managers, customers, distributors, suppliers, competitors, regulators, and society? That is precisely the aim of a statement of corporate responsibility. Such a statement attempts to sort out the relative priority management assigns to each of the company's stakeholders.

In an attempt to please everyone, all too many statements of corporate responsibility turn out to be bland statements about apple pie, motherhood, and the American flag. If a statement of corporate responsibility is to have any real bite, it must take a position as to whether employees, customers, or investors are more important. The entire credibility of the management philosophy will be undermined if the philosophy says one thing but managerial behavior is always antithetical to the stated philosophy. The philosophy should not make gratuitous statements about the impor-

Ukrop's Mission Statement

The mission of Ukrop's Super Markets, Inc. is to serve our customers and community more effectively than anyone else by treating our customers, associates, and suppliers as we personally would like to be treated.

To our customers, we will provide the greatest value possible by offering wide variety and excellent service, while fulfilling our customers' desire for nutritious, high-quality food, uncompromising freshness, and low prices. We will do our best to make their food shopping experience pleasant by providing clean stores, courteous and competent associates, and a friendly, caring attitude.

For our associates, we will promote a pleasant and challenging work environment where work can be an enjoyable experience. We will give our associates an opportunity to grow and advance according to their proven abilities and demonstrated desire to improve themselves professionally. We will fairly compensate our associates for their performance and they will share in the success of the company through profit-sharing bonuses.

To our suppliers, we will do our best to provide a fair return on their investments of time and resources. We will treat suppliers fairly and honestly by striving to meet or exceed their expectations of Ukrop's.

In our community, we will be financially active, returning 10% of our profits to the community to support worthwhile activities. We will encourage our associates to become involved in making our community a better place to live and conduct business. Furthermore, we will continue to seek ways to reuse, recycle, and reduce waste in order to help our environment.

We believe we can best accomplish our mission and achieve profitable growth and long-term financial success by promoting an atmosphere of mutual trust, honesty, and integrity between Ukrop's and our customers, our associates, our suppliers, and our community.

tance of customers and employees unless management is prepared to act accordingly. Among companies which consistently receive high marks for social responsibility are Ben & Jerry's, Campbell Soup, Dayton Hudson, 3M, and Quaker Oats.

Ukrop's is a small, high-quality, upscale supermarket chain located in Richmond, Virginia. Its mission statement is an excellent example of a statement of corporate responsibility with real substance. One need only spend fifteen minutes in any Ukrop's store to observe the high quality of Ukrop's merchandise and the positive, courteous attitude of all employees. As for returning 10 percent of corporate profits to the local community, there is visible evidence of Ukrop's generosity all over the city of Richmond. It also has a very active recycling program. Unlike that of many other companies, Ukrop's mission statement is not a bland, meaningless public relations ploy. Rather it seems to reflect the actual business practices of its owner-managers.

In response to the "anything goes" behavior of many American companies in the 1980s, some individual and private investors began divesting their portfolios of companies that were not socially responsible. A number of so-called socially responsible mutual funds came into existence to meet the needs of more socially minded investors. One such fund that has an impressive financial track record is the Calvert Social Investment Fund.

Every potential investment is first screened for financial soundness and then evaluated according to the Calvert Fund's social criteria. The social criteria identify companies that:

1. *deliver safe products* and services in ways that sustain our natural environment

2. are *managed with participation* throughout the organization in defining and achieving objectives

3. *negotiate fairly* with workers, create an environment supportive of their wellness, and provide options for women, disadvantaged minorities, and others for whom equal opportunities have been denied

4. *foster awareness* of a commitment to human goals, such as creativity, productivity, self-respect, and responsibility, within the organization and the world, and continually

re-create an environment within which these goals can be realized

The Calvert Social Investment Fund does not invest in companies that:

1. engage in business with *oppressive regimes*
2. manufacture *weapon systems*
3. are involved in the production of *nuclear energy*

Workplace Democracy

Even though we take pride in the freedom, individual liberty, and democratic nature of our nation, Kirkpatrick Sale has cogently observed that "during the hours that most of us are employed, we forgo most of our basic democratic rights."[6] In most American companies there are no rights to freedom of speech, freedom of assembly, freedom of the press, or due process. One can be fired on the spot at the whim of one's supervisor without any legal recourse whatsoever.

For most of us, a necessary prerequisite for work to have meaning is an economic and a psychological stake in what we are doing. Two forms of workplace democracy may not only enhance employees' search for meaning but also lead to reduced absenteeism and employee turnover as well as increased productivity. These include *participatory management* and *employee ownership.*

Conspicuously absent in many American firms is a high degree of trust between employees and managers. Yet without two-way trust it is impossible to sustain high levels of productivity. But empowerment is the linchpin of trusting relationships in the workplace. Without empowerment there can be no trust. Employees who do not feel empowered by the organization will not adopt the goals, objectives, and values of the company. To feel empowered, the employees must believe that the managers respect and appreciate their contributions.

One of the reasons why American companies have so much trouble competing with Japanese and European companies is that our growth in productivity has not kept pace with theirs. This reflects, in part, the fact that Japanese and European firms employ management practices which are much more participatory than those used by American companies.

Graduate schools of business have done little to encourage American corporations to become either more participatory or more communitarian. Although most MBA programs require a course in organizational behavior, organizational behavior is often a euphemism for "how to manipulate employees so they will do what we want them to do."

Most American companies employ the same management philosophy today that worked so well for them in the 1950s. However, the typical American worker at that time was not very well educated and grew up during the Great Depression in the 1930s. Today's workers are much better educated, more mobile, and have never known unemployment or poverty. The top-down authoritarian management practices of the 1950s produce alienation, high employee turnover, and declining productivity in the 1990s.

Until recently, managers of authoritarian, hierarchical American companies have shown little interest in sharing power with employees. What is called for is not sweeping new laws to protect the rights of employees, but a strong shift in the thinking of labor and management alike. The key to improved industrial relations lies in increased participation of employees in decision making. We should take a very serious look at employee participation programs in countries such as Austria, Germany, Japan, Sweden, and Finland—shop-floor participation, employee representation on boards of directors, and employee ownership. Corporate and government coercion of American labor have done little to improve our competitiveness abroad.

However, participatory management was dealt a severe blow in Sweden in 1992, when a combination of softness in the global automobile market and the ailing Swedish economy forced Volvo to close two of its three plants. One of the plants to be closed was the renowned Kalmar factory, where Volvo devised its team-assembly approach.

An increasing number of American companies have begun experimenting with participatory management practices, including Eli Lilly, General Electric, Hewlett-Packard, and Motorola. Historically, management has been accustomed to imposing its ideas on company employees rather than drawing on the combined experience of managers and employees. But there are signs that this is beginning to change. There is an increasing awareness on the part of labor and management that adversarial labor-management relations don't pay. The only real winners from our confrontational labor-management practices are our foreign competitors. Neither unreasonable antilabor policies nor irresponsible labor demands for shorter hours, narrow job classifications, and artificial workload limits do much to strengthen America's competitive position in the international marketplace.

Having lost more than one-third of the United States market to foreign competition, it is not surprising that the Big Three automakers have begun to emulate the management practices of their competitors. Each of the Big Three is using team approaches to automobile production, but it may be a case of too little, too late.

Raritan River, Nucor, and Florida Steel have achieved efficiency increases and cost reductions by turning to smaller, mini steel mills. The mini-mills cut costs through participatory management, reduced capital costs, lean corporate staffs, new technologies, location near markets, and concentration on one or two products. Even conservative USX (formerly U.S. Steel) has had some success with participatory management techniques.

To help its employees balance the pressures of work and family life, IBM offered them several new options including leaves of absence of up to three years, greater flexibility in work hours, and a chance for some employees to work at their homes. Chrysler, Kaiser Aluminum, and Weirton Steel now have employee-selected members of their boards of directors.

The ultimate form of communitarian management is the employee-owned company. There are now more than 8,000 employee-owned companies in the United States, the best known of which are United Parcel Service (UPS), Avis, and Chicago Northwestern Railroad. With annual sales of more than $17 billion, UPS is the best known and also the most successful of the employee-owned companies. Known for the reliability of its service and its low-cost rates, UPS is owned by 18,000 of its managers and supervisors. It is by far the most profitable transportation company in the United States. Its founder, James E. Casey, declared that the company must be "owned by its managers and managed by its owners." Through a generous annual bonus plan and an employee stock option plan, employees who began their careers at UPS as clerks and drivers retire as multimillionaires. The employee turnover rate is only 4 percent.

Concerning the benefits of employee ownership, Casey once said,

> There is no bigger incentive than for someone to work for himself. . . . The basic principle which I believe has contributed to the building of our business as it exists today is the ownership of our company by the people employed by it.

Outsourcing

A combination of economic and technological forces has created new possibilities for self-employment in the United States. As the pattern of downsizing begun by large corporations in the late 1980s continued in the 1990s, many companies now hire a significant number of temporary employees, independent consultants, and free lances to do the work previously done by in-house personnel. Personal computer technology has further reenforced this trend. Thousands of individuals are now employed in their homes as independent accountants, financial advisors, travel agents, market researchers, word processors, computer programmers, design engineers, writers, and public relations specialists.

The modern label for this new type of cottage industry is *outsourcing*. Outsourcing enables employers to cut costs and to be more flexible in responding to rapidly changing business conditions. The tools of this emerging new trade are the home computer, the car telephone, and the fax machine. The benefits of this form of self-employment to independent contractors are obvious—flexibility, low overhead, self-actualization, and the chance to be one's own boss. Husbands and wives can share child care and homemaking responsibilities in this type of work environment.

The Mondragon Cooperatives

*B*eginning some forty years ago with a lowly parish priest and several students, people in and around the town of Mondragon in the Basque region of Spain have built a vital, successful and resilient network of more than 170 worker-owned-and-operated cooperatives serving well over 100,000 people. The Mondragon cooperatives include a large worker-controlled bank, worker-self-managed technical as-sistance and research-and-development organizations, a chain of department stores, high-tech firms, appliance manufacturers and machine shops. Despite Franco's repres-sion, economic recessions, and fierce competition, the coop-erative network has created over 21,000 secure and well-paid jobs (losing only three businesses in the process), forged innovative and responsive democratic decision-mak-ing structures, and invented increasingly sophisticated forms of democratic participation, cooperation, and com-munity. What an inspirational and practical model of demo-cratic community economics!

ROY MORRISON
We Build the Road as We Travel

Although outsourcing has created a substantial number of new opportunities for meaningful work, it is not without some serious risks. It is quite possible for these independent operators to end up with no health insurance, few training opportunities, and very limited job security.

Finding Meaningful Employment

From our analysis of the quest for meaning in the workplace, two conclusions emerge. First, finding meaningful work is a diffi-cult undertaking. Second, creating a work environment that will facilitate employees' search for meaning is equally challenging.

Whether one is searching for meaningful employment or attempting to fashion a work environment that will enhance the meaningfulness of employees' work, the answers to seven questions are of fundamental importance:

1. Who is doing the work?
2. How is the work organized?
3. What is the nature of the work?
4. What is the product of the work?
5. Who benefits from the product?
6. Who may be harmed by the production or consumption of the product?
7. How are employees compensated?

If we believe that the search for meaning is somehow connected to the care and nurturing of our soul, then how can we take charge of our soul, if we are marching to the beat of another drummer who tells us what to do, how to do it, and when to do it? No matter what kind of business one may be in, there are endless possibilities for conflict and tension between those who actually do the work and those who manage the enterprise. It is very difficult to be your own boss—to be a free person—if you owe your soul to the company store.

In no sense are we arguing that self-employment is the only means by which one can find meaning in the workplace. In our complex, highly interdependent industrial economy, finding meaning in large organizations, whether they be business, government, or nonprofit enterprises, is not an easy task. No matter what the product may be, multilayered bureaucratic organizations tend to stifle one's search for meaning. If we feel we have no control over our own destiny in a large enterprise, then we may soon become disillusioned and alienated. If employees possess no stake in the enterprise—economically or psychologically—then sustained meaningfulness is impossible to achieve. From an organizational standpoint, employee participation and ownership are of critical importance to the search for meaning in the workplace. Some companies attempt to simulate the benefits of self-employment and employee ownership through communitarian management practices.

Obviously the nature of one's work itself is an important determinant of meaning. Mindless, boring, repetitive clerical or assembly line jobs do little to enhance one's quest for meaning at work. To combat the alienation and meaninglessness associated with factory work, some Japanese companies are trying to make work as fun as possible through the creation of so-called dream factories. In Nissan Motor Company's newest factory, workers toil not in the assembly plant or paint shop, but rather work "happily" in the assembly or painting pavilions. They can walk along Palm Street and over Flamingo Bridge to an employee cafeteria called the Harbor View Restaurant, which has a panoramic view of loading docks. Dream factories are aimed at Japanese young people who have begun shunning assembly-line work because it is viewed as monotonous, fast-paced, and physically exhausting.[7] Ben & Jerry's may not be a "dream company," but it surely comes close.

Whether one's work is meaningful or not also depends on the nature of the fruits of one's labor. If someone is trying to find meaning from being, then it is hard to imagine that working for a company which produces low quality plastic toys and consumer goods could ever prove to be very meaningful. On the other hand, some people might find meaning producing life-saving pharmaceutical products regardless of how boring the work might be. For those who reject nihilism, hand gun and automatic assault weapon production must seem meaningless. Companies that ignore the environmental consequences of their actions are flirting with nihilism.

Some people derive meaning from their work only because it enables them to do something else which is meaningful to them. For example, it is not uncommon to find artists, writers, and musicians who teach in schools or colleges primarily to support their art, writing, and music, respectively. Many journalists write for newspapers so that they can afford to write novels, short stories, or poetry.

How and by whom one is compensated for one's services may also influence the meaningfulness of one's work. Consider, for example, the practice of medicine. In most countries, physicians are paid a salary. In the United States they make more money if their patients are very sick and remain in the hospital for long periods of time. The practice of medicine in our country is primarily a business. For the physician, then, does meaning stem from the service provided to patients or from the money received from them?

Four Strategies for Meaningful Work

1. *Self-employment*—do your own thing.
2. *Employee Ownership*—go to work for an employee-owned company like UPS or Avis.
3. *Participatory Management*—seek employment with an organization which is into power sharing, tension reduction, and other communitarian management practices.
4. *Negotiation*—try to negotiate a more participatory approach to management with your employer.

A popular myth perpetrated by conservative ideologues is that only privately owned profit-making enterprises are efficient and productive. People who work for inefficient, nonprofit enterprises including government are said to be the dregs of society. According to this distorted way of thinking, the only meaningful work which ever takes place is in the private sector. All nationalized companies are thought to be stodgy, bloated, and unimaginative. But this jaundiced view of the world overlooks that outside of England, the former Soviet Union, and Eastern Europe, there are some very successful and very profitable state-owned companies. France is a case in point. The Renault automobile group, the Thompson electronics group, the Rhone-Poulenc chemical company, and Pechiney, the aluminum and packaging giant, are all huge, state-owned companies. Their mandate under the French Socialist government was, "Become profitable or else." The strategies employed by these French state-owned companies differ little from their counterparts in the private sector.

On Work

*W*hat is work? Work is a particular form of conversation between people, which sustains life and enhances human growth. Because of the value of life, work takes on its own meaning and dignity.

JOZEF TISCHNER
Polish Theologian and Solidarity Leader [8]

The search for meaningful employment is no different from the search for meaning elsewhere. The meaning options in the workplace are the same as those depicted in the life matrix—meaninglessness, separation, having, and being. The crafting of our soul in the workplace requires a well-defined sense of direction, discipline, and commitment. The spiritual, intellectual, emotional, and physiological dimensions of our life demand continuous attention both in the workplace and otherwise. Could we ever die happy, if we spent most of our life engaged in work that was utterly meaningless? Work is one of the most important tools in our search for meaning. We now turn our attention to several other tools, which may also be helpful to us in our quest.

_____Chapter 9_____

TOOLS FOR THE SEARCH

But God hath revealed them unto us by his Spirit: for the Spirit searcheth all things, yea, the deep things of God.

1 CORINTHIANS 2:10 KJV

Relatively few of us possess either the will or the psychological sophistication to pursue the search for meaning completely alone, without any outside help. Most of us find it necessary to employ one or more tools to facilitate our search. We shall now examine six such tools:

1. psychotherapy
2. biopsychiatry
3. education
4. literature
5. fine arts
6. religion

Psychotherapy and Biopsychiatry

Some people are so mentally disturbed and psychologically unstable that the search for meaning may be impossible without professional counseling. For those who are mentally ill, psychotherapy and biopsychiatry may prove to be helpful. Those of us who are not mentally ill—or at least think we are not—may also benefit from psychotherapy. We are all searching for a medicine for our separation and meaninglessness and a doctor for our soul.

The main objective of psychotherapy is *engagement*. By raising our level of awareness of what is actually happening in our lives, effective *psychotherapy* not only helps us find meaning but enables us better to evaluate the consequences of our actions. Psychotherapy can teach us how to accept ourselves, love ourselves, and feel respect for ourselves. Without loving ourselves we cannot effectively search for meaning: "Why should I try to find meaning for someone I don't even love?" Psychotherapy can also be used to help us delay gratification, accept responsibility, get in touch with reality, and learn to make trade-offs.

Psychologist Rollo May has suggested that the purpose of psychotherapy is to help us become free to be aware of and experience our possibilities. Through psychotherapy, we are better able to use our freedom to confront or engage our destiny. The role of psychotherapy is through conversation between therapist and client, to teach us *how to be* and *how to become* ourselves, rather than how to possess, manipulate, and control. It helps us confront our existential anxieties—freedom and destiny, isolation and loneliness, and fear of death. A loving psychotherapist can also help us craft our soul.

Psychotherapists heal by listening to another's story. The power of psychotherapy lies in the relationship between the therapist and the patient. Sometimes the only way to heal the patient is by healing the doctor as well.

Psychotherapy can contribute significantly to our search for meaning—particularly by helping us realize that we are responsible for finding our own meaning in life. We cannot expect someone else to find meaning for us. The responsibility rests clearly on our shoulders and not with our parents, teachers, priests, God, or psychotherapist.

The value of the life matrix to psychotherapy lies in the fact that it makes the options available to the patient explicit. We may either succumb to meaninglessness, separation, and having, or we can pursue meaning through *being* and *becoming* who we are. The role of the therapist is to be our trusted mentor and to guide us through the choices—to be our consultant, not a decision maker.

A skilled therapist *helps* us come to terms with meaninglessness and death; confront our separation; contemplate the consequences of a life based on having; seek meaning through being; and write our personal history, philosophy, and strategy. Our search for meaning in the workplace and in community also can be facilitated by a caring therapist. Our therapist may even suggest alternative tools for our quest including education, literature, fine arts, and religion.

Ultimately, the mission of the psychotherapist differs little from that of a priest—to teach us (1) how to be, (2) how to care for our soul, and (3) how to die.

During the decade of the 1980s, *biopsychiatry* or psychopharmacology replaced psychotherapy as the treatment of choice among most psychiatrists. Although no psychiatrist would ever claim that antidepressants, tranquilizers, neuroleptics, or any other drug can provide patients with a sense of meaning, such drugs may nevertheless play useful roles in providing at least temporary stability to the life of the patient so that the search for meaning may begin.

According to Lawrence Hartmann, former President of the American Psychiatric Association, the increased popularity of biopsychiatry reflects the fact that psychiatry has regressed from an integrated *biopsychosocial* model to a narrow physiologically driven *biomedical* model of disease. In the past, although physiological factors were considered by psychiatrists in the treatment of mental illness, psychological and social factors were given more weight than appears to be the case today. The biomedical model assumes disease can be accounted for by deviations from the norm of measurable biological phenomena. This model assumes that mental illness is not influenced by spiritual, emotional, intellectual, or social factors. It combines dualism with reductionism. *Dualism* is the assumption that the mind and the body are completely independent of one another. *Reductionism* assumes that our bodily functions can be analyzed by examining the component parts of each function separately. Bodily functions are thought to be linked by simple cause-and-effect relationships, and diseased components are treated in a linear causal fashion.[1]

There are a number of specific reasons why biopsychiatry has taken on such an important role in psychiatry. First, schizophrenic, biologically depressed, and manic-depressive patients have derived little or no benefit from psychotherapy alone. Second, psychotherapy can be a long, drawn out, highly labor intensive, and expensive process for which insurance companies are increasingly unwilling to pay. Some unscrupulous psychotherapists have exploited their patients by creating an endless dependency relationship with them. Third, there is a very strong economic incentive motivating psychiatrists toward psychopharmacology. The psychiatrist may charge a patient $50 for a fifteen-minute appointment to adjust his or her medication. Obviously, this is much more profitable than a fifty-minute psychotherapy session for which the psychiatrist receives $90. Indeed, some psychiatrists have found that "managing the medication" for patients of psychologists and social workers is so lucrative that they do virtually no psychotherapy at all. Psychopharmacology is a high-volume, high-profit business for those psychiatrists who are more interested in treating the symptoms of their patients than trying to understand the root causes of their problems. Sometimes it is a matter of chance as to whether a particular antidepressant actually relieves the patient's symptoms of pain and suffering.

Drug Addiction

*W*e live in a society which sends poor people to prison for drug addiction. But if you have enough money, your physician and your friendly neighborhood pharmacist will help you meet your every psychopharmacological need—legally, that is.

THE ECONOMIST

Managing the medication for someone else's patients on the basis of a thirty-minute evaluation session is risky business. How is it possible to prescribe mind-altering chemicals with significant side effects for patients you barely know? How well can you adjust the patient's medication on the telephone when you have no idea who the person is on the other end of the line requesting your services?

Fourth, in this age of high technology and instant gratification, few patients are willing to invest the time and money required for long-term psychotherapy. Patients are looking for the quick-fix drug to make them feel better now! Drugs that give patients quick relief from their emotional pain often discourage their search. Such patients frequently respond to medication with, "I feel better now, so I must be O.K." Some psychiatrists are all too willing to accommodate the needs of their "me" generation patients. Since they truly believe they can have it all, the patients assume that medical science can bring instantaneous relief to their existential pain—an assumption which turns out not to be true. Prescribing medication gives physicians a greater feeling of power and control than is the case with psychotherapy.

Consider the case of Evelyn, a thirty-five-year-old woman admitted to the hospital for treatment of depression, with a history of physical abuse by her husband. To help her depression and insomnia, she was treated with Elavil, an antidepressant with strong sedative properties. Her sleep improved, but she continued to feel depressed, and her energy level remained low, so her physician prescribed another antidepressant, Prozac. Since Evelyn still felt lethargic, she was given Ritalin. Lithium then was added for her mood swings. When her anxiety level increased—no doubt influenced by the side effects of the four drugs she was already taking—Ativan was prescribed. Thus we have a patient who was admitted to the hospital with depression being treated with five different medications for five different symptoms: depressed mood, insomnia, low energy, mood swings, and anxiety.

In his book *Darkness Visible,* novelist William Styron describes his bout with deep depression. His conclusion after several months of improperly administered medication was that many psychiatrists "maintain their stubborn allegiance to pharmaceuticals in the belief that eventually the pills will kick in, the patient will respond, and the somber surroundings of the hospital will be avoided."[2]

Interestingly enough, there are a few signs suggesting that at least some psychiatrists feel that the pendulum has swung too far in the high-tech physiological direction in psychiatry. Hartmann has called for a return to the biopsychosocial model, which integrates more humane values into psychiatry. In the past, not only were many psychiatrists and psychologists practicing atheists and agnostics, but they were very hostile even to mentioning religion in the context of psychotherapy. However, Daniel Goleman reports in the *New York Times* that there is increased awareness among mental health professionals of the importance of the spiritual needs of their patients.[3] Some psychotherapists are now actually encouraging their patients to talk about their religious beliefs and their spiritual emptiness.

> *I* am very concerned that psychiatrists are ignoring their own spiritual lives. The biggest part of being a therapist is working on yourself.
>
> M. SCOTT PECK, M.D.[4]

We believe there is a definite need for an existential psychotherapeutic paradigm which goes well beyond simplistic Freudian analysis and mechanistic biopsychiatry. Such a paradigm would integrate into the psychotherapeutic process the seven-step search for meaning outlined in chapter 1, including the life matrix and our personal history, philosophy, and strategy. The workplace, community, education, literature, fine arts, and religion would be an integral part of this paradigm. There have been few new developments since Irvin D. Yalom's path-breaking *Existential Psychotherapy*, published in 1980.[5]

Education

Our search began in earnest with a course, "The Search for Meaning," a course unlike most others offered within the university. It evolved out of our concern that, to paraphrase Walker Percy, people were "making all A's in school but flunking life."

Education ought to be a continual, lifelong affair, an indispensable tool in the search. Defined as the systematic, purposeful effort to transmit, evoke, or acquire knowledge, attitudes, skills, or values, education is at the heart of the search. However, there are problems with the way most of us have experienced education.

For one thing, when most of us think "education" we think "school." When you were around six, you were taken away from your family and handed over to strangers, people who were paid to educate you, as if that was not what was already going on in your life. These people, the teachers and principals in your elementary school, were presumed to know something about learning which everyone else did not. They were professionals. So immediately, right at the first, you got the impression that education is something done by someone else to you or for you. Furthermore, in school, we put you in a group. We demanded that everyone in the group pay attention, remain quiet, still, and move at the same rate.

Even though we know that people do *not* learn in the same way, do *not* learn at the same rate, that chronological age has little to do with where a person is in relationship to ability to learn, schools keep treating education *en masse*. There is a reason for this apparent disregard for human intellectual development. Our schools were designed to prepare people to work in factories, to inculcate the skills necessary to work well on Mr. Ford's assembly lines. On the farm, no one had to worry about clocks. Work began when the sun rose and ended when it went down. Most agricultural labor is not closely interlocked. But in the factory, clocks were essential because everyone must be on time, standing in position ready to begin when the whistle blows. Assembly-line production makes uniformity, punctuality, ability to follow directions, and compliant efficiency the supreme virtues. Schools, which educate for the assembly line, have bells which ring on the hour, put great stress on everyone's moving efficiently from class to class, staying in line, following the rules. Our friends Johnny and Sasha were educated in schools like these.

Perhaps such schooling worked well in the 1920s. Perhaps it made sense then. Unfortunately, it makes little sense now in an economy which increasingly demands creativity, individual initiative, and personal responsibility. Tragically, most of our schools plod along as if nothing has happened. Our schools manage to look more like factories than factories, to crank out people who are well equipped for a world that no longer exists. After attending schools that stifle their imagination and creativity, our children then go on to colleges and universities, which were designed to provide, for all but a few, little more than a set of skills for a vocation which could have been acquired more easily through work experience or apprenticeship.

Most tragic for the search for meaning, schooling tends to nullify education as a tool in the search for meaning. Passivity, uniformity, and mere punctuality were not helpful virtues in the search. Too many of us, by the time our formal schooling is over, have learned only one lesson by heart—education is boring and irrelevant, and its purpose is mainly to convince us of all that we do *not* know rather than invite us to search for all that we *can* know.

Each of us therefore must be "deschooled" in order to continue our education. We must become savvy in how we best learn, under what conditions we assimilate information and gain new insights and understandings. It is often noted that the word *educare*, the root of "education," can mean either to "bring out" or to "bring up." Education can be a process of bringing out insights within us, a reconstruction of our experience in which we see things in a new and life-changing way. This type of education assumes that the learner brings to the educational task certain experiences and concepts, which can be used for growth. It realizes that each learner is different. Education as leading out will take the form of a process of unfolding rather than a program of indoctrination. It will be open-ended, always open to that "teachable moment" when things "click" in the mind and experience of the learner and transformation occurs.

Education can also mean to "bring up." This type of education does not shy away from indoctrination, the process whereby an experienced person passes on information or insights to one with less experience. Formation is its goal, the acquisition of skills and information. This type of education is most popular in the sciences or the arts, but it is a widely held view in all branches of education. Most of our schools are better at formation than transformation. As we noted, education that is exclusively formative in nature, "bringing up" rather than "bringing out," tends to promote passivity in the learner, the impression that wisdom is a set of information "out there," which must simply be inculcated "in here" and then "I'm done."

In many of our seminars, people tell us that they found that their most important education began *after* they left school. We often say things like, "Education is wasted on the young." By that we may mean, not that the young are incapable of learning, but rather with schools in the state they are in, the search only begins after formal, state-sanctioned education has done its worst with us and we are at last set free to learn life.

Several nonfiction books have been particularly helpful to us in our own journey of search and discovery. We recommend them to you.

Search Bibliography

1. Becker, Ernest. *The Denial of Death.* New York: Free Press, 1973.
2. Camus, Albert. *The Myth of Sisyphus.* New York: Alfred A. Knopf, 1955.
3. ———. *The Rebel.* New York: Alfred A. Knopf, 1956.
4. Frankl, Viktor E. *Man's Search for Meaning.* New York: Washington Square Press, 1984.
5. Fromm, Erich. *To Have or To Be.* New York: Bantam, 1981.
6. May, Rollo. *Freedom and Destiny.* New York: Dell, 1981.
7. Peck, M. Scott. *The Road Less Traveled.* New York: Touchstone, 1978.
8. Tillich, Paul. *The Courage to Be.* New Haven, Conn.: Yale University Press, 1952.
9. Yalom, Irvin D. *Existential Psychotherapy.* New York: Basic Books, 1980.

Literature

Literature, the reading of novels and poetry, can be a valuable tool in our search for meaning. At its best, literature is a mirror to life. The greatest early novelists, the veritable inventors of the novel, were women. In the novel, we are given access to the intimate lives of others. We have the opportunity to act out modes of living and acting that are different from those we have in life. We peer over someone else's shoulder as that person makes decisions and lives them through to their consequences. A novelist like Jane Austen, who never traveled more than a few miles from her home during her entire life, puts the human psyche under a microscope and thereby shows us aspects of life we would have missed if we had been left to our own devices.

Good literature, unlike bad literature, shows us how difficult it is to be honest, how caught we are in a web of our own devising. With Flaubert's Emma Bovary, we dream of romance and adventure only to have our dreams dissolve into dust. We are shocked by Flannery O'Connor's crazy characters, only to see ourselves and those we love in their craziness.

Bad literature, unlike good literature, only parrots back to us our worst illusions about ourselves. Rather than see or experience our lives in new ways, we are left to bathos, sentimentality. Iris Murdoch once called good literature "a kind of goodness by proxy." Good literature helps us to see, and, if we can see clearly, we can live more meaningfully.

One of us had this experience a few years ago. Grounded in a distant airport in a snowstorm, I wandered into the airport bookstore, purchasing the largest book for the lowest price, Tolstoy's *War and Peace,* the sort of book I was supposed to read in college but had neither the time nor the inclination to do so. For the next fifteen hours, I read *War and Peace,* entirely immersed in its characters and the events of their lives. When the plane finally landed at my home airport many pages and hours later and I laid the book aside, I was a different person. My world had been rearranged. I now saw things in myself and my world I had missed before. I was living somewhere different from where I began the book. I had achieved a kind of wisdom by proxy.

In our class, we read Anne Tyler's *Saint Maybe,* a story of a young man named Ian. After unknowingly assisting in the suicide of his brother and eventually the death of his brother's wife, Ian decides to drop out of college and rear his dead brother's children. Our students confessed a great initial discomfort and even anger when they began reading Ian's story. After all, they, like Ian, were college freshmen. They had cast their lot with college, considering it to be the most important task they could be giving their lives to at that moment. Yet here was a book that told about a young man who felt compelled to turn his back on that life. By the end of *Saint Maybe,* the students said they had a new appreciation for the richness of life's possibilities. College, career, profession were important, but perhaps not all important. Anne Tyler had opened the door for them and shown them a new world. They were now different people. That is the sort of thing literature can do for us.

A Drunkard's Walk

WHEN I SURVEY THE THRUST AND PRODUCT,
                           THE GRAY SLAG WASTE
          OF MY PAST DAYS
AND RECONJURE TIME ABANDONED TO HOPE
                           AND VISION'S INTENSITY,
               I SEE A SHADOW TRAIL
                           THAT WEAVES AND TWISTS
          AMONG PHANTOM GRAILS,
     A DRUNKARD'S WALK
               THROUGH FAILED SUCCESSES,
     TAKEN   IN   LOVE   TO AMUSE,   DISTRACT   —TO GRANDLY
ACHIEVE,
       THAT   ALWAYS   FASCINATE,   PALE   THEN   LEAVE.

                    BUT
               ANOTHER SHAPE
               BEHIND THIS WALK
     BEYOND THE ABSURDITY OF ITS FIGURE
          CLOSER THAN I AM TO ME
          REDEEMS THE PHANTOM GRAILS,
     TRANSFIGURES THE LOST SUCCESSES
     ALIGNS THE STAGGER OF THIS JOURNEY.

                                        JACK A. DeLOYHT

Irvin D. Yalom's novel, *When Nietzsche Wept,* is the story of a fictional encounter between German philosopher Friedrich Nietzsche and eminent Viennese physician Josef Breuer in 1882. Nietzsche and Breuer strike a bargain in which Breuer agrees to be Nietzsche's physician for one month, treating his migraine headaches and other physical ailments, in return for Nietzsche's acting as the doctor of Breuer's soul. Both men suffer from a common obsession with women triggered by their own despair—separation, meaninglessness, and fear of growing old and dying. In the end, both Nietzsche and Breuer are healed by concentrating their attention on the other.

In his best-selling book *The Closing of the American Mind,* Allan Bloom suggests that the meaninglessness felt by American college students may be linked to their lack of knowledge of the work of great philosophers and writers such as Socrates, Plato, Machiavelli, Rousseau, and Kant. Colleges and universities can do more to help their students with the search. In addition to providing them with a firm grounding in classical philosophy and literature, they can also expose them to novels such as Albert Camus's *The Stranger* and *The Plague,* Franz Kafka's *The Trial* and *The Castle,* Milan Kundera's *The Unbearable Lightness of Being,* and Walker Percy's *The Moviegoer* and *The Thanatos Syndrome,* as well as plays like Arthur Miller's *Death of a Salesman,* Eugene O'Neill's *The Iceman Cometh,* Jean-Paul Sartre's *The Flies* and *No Exit,* and Tennessee Williams' *A Streetcar Named Desire.*

Fine Arts

Painting, sculpture, dance, drama, music, and film also can be a mirror to life, though sometimes less immediately relevant to the search for meaning. Through the fine arts we probe those feelings and insights too deep for words. One of our students spent the whole semester never speaking a word in class. In the oral exam, he had great difficulty putting his thoughts into speech. He casually mentioned that he sometimes "fooled around with a little painting." When we expressed interest, he brought in one of his paintings. It was a deeply moving, yet somber, depiction of a group of people with one person standing off to the side, detached, apart from the group. The student was able to paint what he could not say in words.

A symphony begins with great melodic effect. But then the music moves in unexpected directions. Counter melodies are heard. The ear wants to linger and enjoy some of the movements of the symphony longer, but the orchestra moves on to explore heights and depths of feeling. The tempo begins a crescendo, then returns to the originating theme. What does this music do to the listener of the symphony? In what ways do these themes and counter themes, the search for a memorable melody, correspond to life?

On Art

*A*rt uncovers a profound sense of life and gives life a new meaning. Art shows life in a different, deeper light. Poetry is a kind of art which can "transform paupers into angels" (Juliusz Slowacki).

JOZEF TISCHNER[6]

Both art and literature are a response to meaninglessness and despair, according to Paul Tillich and Albert Camus. In Tillich's words, "The creators of modern art have been able to see the meaninglessness of our existence; they participated in its despair. At the same time they have had the courage to face it and to express it in their pictures and sculptures. They had the courage to be as themselves."[7] Camus goes so far as to suggest that the search for meaning is the driving force underlying all forms of art: "I ought not to have written: if the world were clear, art would not exist—but if the world seemed to me to have a meaning I should not write at all."[8]

Ingmar Bergman's classic film, *The Seventh Seal,* is a stunning allegory about humankind's search for meaning. A medieval knight returning home from the Crusades through plague-stricken Europe encounters Death, who sportingly agrees to a chess game. Hanging in the balance are the lives of the knight and an innocent group of traveling players. *The Seventh Seal* is a timeless observation of humanity's optimism and a lasting tribute to the genius of Bergman. The search for meaning was a common theme in most of Bergman's films of the 1950s and 1960s, as well as in the 1982 film *Fanny and Alexander.*

Popular televison producer Norman Lear often bases his situation comedies on the quest for meaning. Archie Bunker, the hero of Lear's popular series "All in the Family," was an alienated blue-collar worker with deep-rooted emotional and spiritual problems.

The Artist and the Rebel

The artist reconstructs the world to his plan. The symphonies of nature know no rests. The world is never quiet; even its silence eternally resounds with the same notes, in vibrations that escape our ears. . . . Music exists, however, in which symphonies are completed, where melody gives its form to sounds that by themselves have none, and where, finally, a particular arrangement of notes extracts from natural disorder a unity that is satisfying to the mind and the heart.

ALBERT CAMUS
The Rebel [9]

Modern life tends to anesthetize us. We become numb to real pleasure or true pain. Finding a workable routine, we continue in our assigned ruts, one day after the other. From what we have observed, meaning arises in those people's lives who are continually willing to expose their lives to the creative contributions of others. Indeed, we wonder if some people's sense of life's meaninglessness may only be a testimony of their lack of exposure to the contributions of others who have more fully given themselves to the task of analyzing and experiencing the richness of life.

Cha-no-yu and the Art of Aesthetic Living

In Japan an entire art form has evolved around the simple process of serving tea. This art form, called cha-no-yu or the tea ceremony, has been refined over centuries by some of the greatest minds in Japan. Hence, the tea ceremony contains no gratuitous motions. It represents the zenith of efficiency. Every action is purposeful, performed with complete attention and care. In Cha-no-yu, no inner truth is outwardly manifested. Form is not inferior to content. Form is content.

This focus on executing the well-practiced and

---

deliberately paced motions of the tea ceremony is said to temporarily induce a clarity of thought seldom achieved. It supposedly heightens our creativity, and our ability to appreciate the aesthetics of even the most basic human actions. Imagine, for a moment, living a life where every action is purposeful, every thought is clear, and every object and action replete with meaning. It is a high standard to achieve. Masters of the tea ceremony spend whole lifetimes trying to attain it. Yet even one year of living like this would render life more meaningful than it is now.

I believe it is possible to live this way, to live a life of meaning. Why can't washing the dishes or doing the laundry, processes just as simple as serving tea, become acts of artistry? Why can't we strive for purposefulness and efficiency in all of our actions, regardless of their seeming insignificance? All acts of daily life can be rendered meaningful when they are performed with care and attention. In keeping with God as the unconscious, we should do the best we can at everything, thereby learning from it and becoming better as a result. Then and only then, can we lead the aesthetic life.

In living a life of purposeful action, we perpetuate the mind set of the cha-no-yu into all aspects of existence. We maintain an active mind of calm alertness, that never ceases to observe, innovate and analyze. This activity of the mind is of the utmost importance. It signifies that we are living in the true sense of the word. To live we must maintain an active mind, acknowledging that human life at its bare bones is a stream of consciousness, that our ability to focus this consciousness, and carry out the physical actions it intends, is all we have control over. Therefore, when we fail to apply our consciousness, we have failed to think, and thus ceased to live.

This condemnation is not as harsh as it seems. People without active minds miss out on many meaningful aspects of reality. It is saddening, for as Thomas Carlyle wrote, " The tragedy of life is not so much what men can suffer, but rather what they miss." When we partake of the active mind, we miss out on nothing. Our full attention is directed toward all that we do. We do not merely see objects like the absent-minded spectator, passing them by without regard to form or function. We observe intensely and curiously. Consciousness penetrates our view. We comprehend those around us through the subtlety of facial expression, the look of an eye, or the tone of a voice. Through observation and awareness, we grasp the complex truths of life. The average person who seldom thinks cannot do all this, and allows reality to go unappreciated. Simply stated, to think is to live, and live meaningfully.

The mind set of the cha-no-yu allows continual thought. It heightens our perceptions and desecrates the hierarchy of meaningful acts. Life is no longer divided into those actions which are meaningful and those which are not. We cease living our life in anticipation of weekends and vacations, dreading the work week, the traffic, and the endless tasks necessary to maintain life and property. We no longer regard graduations and weddings as the only significant and memorable events in our life. Every "now" of the present possesses purpose and exudes meaning. All of life becomes of consequence.

KENDRA HUDSON
First Year Duke Student

Recently one of us had a very demanding, difficult day with a score of irritations and conflicts. By the end of the day, the job, the coworkers, life itself seemed rather frustrating and pointless. That night I went reluctantly to a concert simply because we had already purchased the tickets and had promised that we would go.

It was an organ concert, the sort of evening where one could relax and let the music surround one. Despite the day's frustrations and vexations, the music managed to lift my spirits, to make me glad to be alive, indeed, glad to be a member of the human race as long as there were people like Bach to be human with. Music had led to meaning.

Religion

No matter how much we understand of life, there is always a surplus of meaning, something still there beyond our understanding, waiting to be understood. Despite our best research, our most adept science, the world cannot be known by laying it on a table and picking it apart as a cadaver. Something more is there. Just when we get the world all figured out, reality fixed and tied down, something intrudes—an event we had not expected, an insight quite outside our capacities, something delightful or terrible we could not have devised—and we realize that more is going on in the present moment than we know. Reality is thick, impervious to simple definitions, ambiguous. There is always more. The primary way for human beings to attempt to describe, to stand in awe of, to plead with, rage against, make peace with that more-than-we-can-know-or-understand is called religion.

Freud claimed that religion was an illusion, a disguised reappearance of unconscious parent-child conflicts. It seems never to have occurred to Freud that our projections of parent-child relationships may nevertheless be human foreshadowing of objectively real God-person relationships. Nietzsche thought that, whenever death becomes our chief concern, religion will become our chief means of dealing with life. Yet death is a fact. Why is religion any less realistic a means of dealing with death than any other means of dealing with death? Any purely naturalistic explanation of human life, such as that attempted by Freud, collides with our awareness that more is going on in us and in our world than can be circumscribed by naturalistic explanations. We know, in our heart of hearts, or in our deepest thoughts, or on the basis of our most significant and secret experiences, there is more.

Marx said that religion was little more than the common person's opium, a means of dulling the pain of economic exploitation. When people are exploited, religion has been a means not only of taking away some of the pain but also of empowering the exploited to live with hope and dignity. On the other hand, for every oppressed person who was dulled into quiescence by religion, count-

On Physical Activity

In general, I have always subscribed to the Oscar Wilde approach to physical exertion. "Occasionally," said Wilde, "I get the urge to engage in physical activity. But if I lie quietly for a time, the urge will pass."

Thus far in our quest for meaning, we have made the search appear to be exclusively cerebral, intellectual, a matter of better thought and analysis. Alas, we three are academics who are victims of the academic penchant to separate mind from body.

The Hebrews made no body-soul dichotomy. Body, mind, and spirit were one piece, a unity. For many of us, the search for meaning will involve a new recognition that we are not disembodied minds or souls. We have a body. What affects us physically affects our spirit as well. Some of us are in psychological or spiritual trouble because we are in physical trouble. We are beings with feelings and ideas, but we also have hormones, muscles, aches, and pains.

I left work the other day depressed and discouraged. There had been conflict, unresolved problems, a host of annoyances. Something in me felt an uncharacteristic need for a vigorous run through the neighborhood. I gave in to the urge. After less than thirty minutes, I was sweating, gasping for breath, but also free, at peace, exhilarated. Nothing had changed at work, yet *I* had changed.

How many of life's difficulties would be resolved with greater attention to our bodies? We don't know. The line between the *psyche* and the *soma* is notoriously thin. Much that we are conditioned to treat through drugs and talk could be treated through aerobics. Some physicians estimate that three-fourths of all hospital patients are there for life-style reasons rather than from simple infection or disease.

If you could have heard one of our students talk about what playing the cello did for her life—the demands the cello made upon her posture, her breathing, her fingers and powers of concentration—you would see how clearly the body affects the soul.

So perhaps the search could be facilitated by your putting down this book and taking a walk.

THE PASTOR

Erikson on Religion

*R*eligion . . . elaborates on what feels profoundly true
even though it is not demonstrable; it translates into significant words, images, and codes the exceeding darkness
which surrounds man's existence and the light which pervades it beyond all desert or comprehension.

E. H. ERIKSON[10]

---

less more were energized to rebel, revolt, to question the present
order on the basis of a higher order. Religion gives little comfort
to human tyrants, for religion points to the ways and means of God,
which transcend human standards.

Vaclav Havel claims that with the collapse of communism the
modern world has ended and at last the whole world has been
forced to recognize that something more is going on than merely
our science, our politics, and our cause-and-effect explanations.
According to Havel, this era has been dominated by the belief that
human beings are "capable of objectively describing, explaining
and controlling everything that exists, and of possessing the one
and only truth of the world."[11] He goes on to say that,

> we have to abandon the arrogant belief that the world is merely a puzzle
> to be solved, a machine with instructions for use waiting to be discov-
> ered, a body of information to be fed into a computer in the hope that,
> sooner or later, it will spit out a universal solution. . . . We must try
> harder to understand than to explain.[12]

He urges politicians to pay more attention to spirituality, the
soul, firsthand insight, and being—a tall order for most politicians.

William James said that religion was what each of us did with
our solitude. For most of us, in most of our religion, James has not
said enough about what it feels like to be religious. Most religion
is a group thing, communal, drawing us closer to our fellow men
and women rather than separating us. Religion, in holding a
higher or deeper concept of human good than that which is
instinctively available to us, contributes to the quest for a more just

society. In joining our voices in prayer or song with others, losing ourselves in the words and moves of religious ritual, we find ourselves caught up in something considerably larger than ourselves. Our present is linked to generations who have come before us. We are coaxed into confronting matters which, in the humdrum of daily life, we too easily avoid.

Alfred North Whitehead declared that

> religion is a vision of something which stands beyond, behind and within the passing flux of things, something which is real and yet waiting to be realized; something which is a remote possibility and yet the greatest of present facts; something that gives meaning to all that passes and yet eludes apprehension; something whose possession is the final good and yet is beyond all reach; something which is the ultimate ideal and yet the hopeless quest.[13]

Admittedly, religion can be infantile, a denial of the facts of life, a polishing of our idealized self-image, an escape from the ugly realities of life into a cozy interior world. Yet this is more of a betrayal of religion than its purpose. Within every religion, there is a capacity for self-critique, a process of refashioning of the self, an impetus toward growth and discovery. Through religion, even the most ordinary aspects of life are given new and deeper significance. We come to believe that our little lives are caught up in some larger purpose, that the world is more than cause-and-effect determinism.

Socrates, who said that he knew very little about God (which may, in reality, show that he knew a very great deal about God), nevertheless called his fellow citizens of Athens to a pilgrimage toward meaning. Obsessed with the notion that reality is deeper than that which we first perceive, that there is meaning beneath and beyond our immediate understanding, Socrates invited the people of Athens to search with him, to join in soul crafting: "Citizens of Athens," asked Socrates, "are not you ashamed to care so much about making all the money you can and advancing your reputation and prestige, while for truth and wisdom and the improvement of your souls you have no thought or care?"

Christian Meaning

For the person who is religious, religion is considerably more than a "tool" for finding meaning, a helpful technique toward a more meaningful life. The religious person, through the rites and practices of his or her faith, is making a large claim about the world: The world really is a place created and sustained by God. For Christians, that God has a face, a name—*Jesus.* The Christian claims that meaning in life is more than a subjectively derived, existentially achieved invention. Meaning is a *gift* of a gracious God who does not leave us to our own devices. Meaning in life is not the result of our own conjuring. God reveals Godself to us, graciously, generously through our scriptures, in the life, death, and resurrection of Jesus, in the prodding and support of sisters and brothers in the church. The meaning we find in life is therefore as much a gift as a discovery. We call it grace. Christian meaning is peculiar—tied to the stories, saints, practices and claims called Christian. It is personal— God's relationship to each of us. It is cosmic—an experience of the very nature of a created and purposeful universe. It is communal—an intergenerational, communally derived gift of those who have passed this way before us. One reason why the search for meaning is so important to Christians is to help us recognize such gifts when they are bestowed upon us. Then to call these gifts "grace," then to call the grace "amazing."

THE PASTOR

Chapter 10

SOUL CRAFTING

If there is a soul, it is a mistake to believe that it is given us fully created. It is created here, throughout a whole life.

ALBERT CAMUS
NOTEBOOKS 1942–1951

When we began our voyage of discovery and found ourselves isolated on a deserted island, we took a somewhat detached, objective view of the meaning options available to us—meaninglessness, separation, having, and being. We are free to choose any source of meaning that we so desire. But as we worked our way through the life matrix, considered our longing for community, contemplated meaninglessness in the workplace, and examined alternative tools to facilitate our search, being emerged as our only real choice. Only through being is it possible to achieve harmony and balance in the spiritual, intellectual, emotional, and physiological dimensions of our life.

The search for meaning is a search for grounding—a sense of connectedness to ourselves, to others, to history, to nature, and to the ground of our being. Our search combines a trip *inward* with an *outward* journey integrated by our soul.

Taking Responsibility for Our Soul

The bottom line of the search for meaning is soul crafting—the care and nurturing of our soul, possibly our only salvage from death's oblivion. Our soul is the sum of our deeds, our work, our creations, our experience, our love, our joy, our pain, and our suffering. Throughout our entire life, our soul is continuously in the process of becoming.

We not only possess the ability to bestow meaning on our life, but we also have the responsibility to do so. The adage, "I am the captain of my ship; the master of my soul,"[1] need *not* be an expression of unabashed paganism and radical individualism, but rather a statement of free will combined with a statement of personal responsibility. Although we are free to choose the meaning of our life, the responsibility for crafting our soul is inescapable. How do we take care of our soul? How do we fine tune it? We do so by being—by caring, loving, sharing, creating, and suffering. To teach ourselves how to be, we seek help from community, the workplace, psychotherapy, education, literature, fine arts, and religion.

Our soul embodies our personal philosophy—our sense of meaning, our values, our ethical principles, and our sense of social responsibility. It is the sum of our joys and sorrows, our hopes and fears, and our goals, objectives, and strategies. It reflects who we are and who we want to become. Our image of what we want the world to become also resides deep within our soul.

Religion and Our Soul

Ultimately, our religion is defined by our stance toward meaninglessness, separation, having, and being. By teaching us how to be, how to relate to others, how to care for our soul, and how to die, religion also teaches us how to live. Religion provides the spiritual basis for our search as well as the care and nurturing of our soul.

Unfortunately, all too many Sunday morning homilies are pitched to those who want to hear syrupy sweet sermons promising zero-cost peace of mind and blissful life after death. Rarely are they disappointed. American churches exist in a buyer's market. Customers must be kept happy. However, by playing to the segment of the congregation which has long since abandoned the search, ministers, priests, and rabbis drive away many thoughtful people who are turned off by unsubstantiated promises of pie in the sky and instant self-esteem. Tragically, these are the people who are often most capable of giving religious institutions new vision and much-needed energy. However, they are alienated by the authoritarian clergy and the superficiality of many churches and synagogues.

Soul Craft

Come by here,
Strange place I affirm
Familiar
Endow with invariance
By firm hold or
Better passionate embrace
Of what may well be dear delusions
Some shared with you
Others' individual fire
Serves to lock them
In joy and pain
Uniquely mine
I built it as I came here
I build it as I go along
From its standpoint
Perseverance
Beyond my body's term
Grounded as it may be
In those dear delusions
Is problematic
That is mostly pain
Hardly joyous in any sense
Except to be with you
In every sense
Continue to build
This place as best we can
Until the problem
Goes away

JACK A. DeLOYHT

Churches are lured into the same bigger-is-better, and growth-at-any-price mentality that afflicts American businesses. The "successful church" is the congregation which keeps the maximum number of people busy in yoga classes, ceramics groups, youth trips to Disney World, and the constant care and feeding of denominational programs. Worship is a preacher-choir performance for passive spectators. A conspiracy of niceness pervades the congregation in which everyone is smiling, everyone is friendly, happy—successful at appearing happy and successful. Talk appears to be about everything except what really matters. Deep, honest, open discussions of meaning are avoided. Persons who honestly confess to the superficiality of their own lives, the meaninglessness of their everyday existence are treated like pariahs, failures at the main business of the church—being happy and successful, or at least appearing to be so on Sunday.

A man in one of our groups, a recovering alcoholic, said that, after his life-changing experience in Alcoholics Anonymous, his local church was unbearable.

> After I had at last been part of a real community where we loved each other enough to be honest, to sacrifice our time and energy to aid others in their struggle with alcohol, the sweet superficiality of my church was repulsive. When I tried to share with them some of the insights gained from my own struggles, they looked at me like I was crazy, like my struggle was a purely personal problem.

The great religious books of the world—the Bible, the Koran, the Vedas—all have much to say about the search for meaning. Yet what they have to say is not simple. Consider the Bible. As we have noted, the biblical books of Ecclesiastes and Job say "Everything is meaningless." The Bible is replete with stories of homicide, violence, and war, many of which are grounded in nihilism. On the other hand, the story of Jesus Christ is a story about being. But the price Jesus paid for a life based on love and community was crucifixion—an act of supreme nihilism. Crucifixion was then followed by resurrection—a sign of the triumph of being.

The very form of the Bible's literature, its complexity and richness, the way it frustrates those who look for simple answers and quick solutions to life's questions, renders the Bible of great value in the search for meaning. In the Bible, God has many faces. We think we know God, have God all figured out for ourselves, nailed down, only to discover a different face of God on the next page. Biblical people are no less complex than the biblical God. In the Bible, we encounter real people, people who are more than cardboard heroes or plaster saints. They are people like Abraham, who had family troubles but who also heard a promise of God; like Joseph and his brothers, who *really* had family troubles but also a dream; like Peter, who meant to be faithful to Jesus but had great difficulty living up to his commitments. And the Bible claims that *these* are the people whom God uses to work his will in the world, these stumbling, inspiring, inept people who look suspiciously like us.

Doubting Thomas

*H*ow often have you heard a minister or a priest stand in the pulpit and express any serious doubts about God, Jesus Christ, the Resurrection, the Trinity, or life after death? Why can't the clergy be more honest and admit that they too have doubts about the answers to life's tough questions? By promising a lot less and being more open about the mysteries of life, churches and synagogues might substantially increase their influence. While the clergy possess no final answers to life's difficult questions, they often are committed to the search and can help others with their own individual searches by encouraging them to express their doubts about the conventional wisdom.

THE ECONOMIST

We modern people want our knowledge pure, distilled, reduced to three or four simple assertions. That's not the way the Bible deals with God or life. Through stories, seemingly contradictory assertions, history, poetry, strange events, the Bible beckons us on a risky, adventurous journey. Frustrating our lust for simple answers to touchy questions, the Bible forces us to choose between seemingly conflicting alternatives, makes us step back from life and consider our path, teases us out beyond our certitude into a world which is at the same time both more confusing and infinitely more interesting than we first imagined.

The Bible (like other great religious books) can be a valuable partner in the search for meaning. Reading honestly, with a playful willingness to be challenged by the Bible, questioned by the Bible, even confused by it, modern people can enter a world much more diverse and real than our reductionistic, flattened landscape modernity has offered us.

Who Is God?

I will never know who God is, or what God is, or even if God is, but I could know that we all have the possibility of being led over more deeply into the mysteries that we identify with God.

THE REVEREND JAMES R. ADAMS, RECTOR
St. Mark's Episcopal Church
Washington, D.C.

We believe that churches and synagogues are well positioned to help their members with their individual searches. A huge spiritual vacuum is waiting to be filled by religious institutions who once again see themselves as essential for the search. Members of churches and synagogues ought to be honest in admitting our willingness to use our religious institutions overly to simplify our lives, to hand us pat answers to tough questions, to give over our God-given freedom into the hands of others. Clergy also need to be honest in admitting their fears at honestly joining with their people in asking tough questions, penetrating the mysteries of life and death, and constructing a more meaningful future for ourselves. What if every church, every religious community set as a goal for itself, the honest confrontation with its members' lack of meaning in their lives and the bold, adventurous communal quest for meaning?

Hear, O Israel: The LORD is our God, the LORD alone. You shall love the LORD your God with all your heart, and with all your soul, and with all your might. Keep these words that I am commanding you today in your heart. (Deut. 6:4-6)

Living with What We Know

The only thing certain about life after death is the complete uncertainty surrounding death itself. What happens when we die? Will we return to this Earth—reincarnated in a different form? Is there a heaven or a hell? Or do we simply die—never to be heard from again? Those who claim to have simple, easy answers to these questions are trying to mislead either themselves or others.

Over and over again Camus admonishes us to live only with what we know rather than what we want to believe about life, death, God, and life after death. No matter how many near-death or out-of-body experiences we may have heard about, life on the other side of the mountain after death remains a great unknown. Life after death, heaven, hell, reincarnation, and nothingness are among the possibilities awaiting us on the other side of the mountain.

Disbelief

*O*ut of disbelief one can create a code of behavior for man, a new morality, a new enlightenment, to replace one born out of superstition and the lust for the supernatural.

IRVIN D. YALOM
When Nietzsche Wept[2]

Regardless of how much anguish admitting it may cause us, many of our perceptions of life after death are based on little more than idle speculation and wishful thinking. Not only do we possess no knowledge of life after death, but our ability to influence it is beyond comprehension.

Whether or not we believe there is another world to which we are held accountable depends on our particular religious faith. But regardless of our religion, can we avoid accountability to ourselves and the rest of the human race? Although Camus did not believe in any life after death, he did not deny accountability in this life. "I do not believe there is another world in which we shall have to 'render account.' But we already have our account to render in this world—to all those we love."[3]

Christian Accountability

*T*hen he will say to those at his left hand, "You that are accused, depart from me into the eternal fire prepared for the devil and his angels; for I was hungry and you gave me no food, I was thirsty and you gave me nothing to drink, I was a stranger and you did not welcome me, naked and you did not give me clothing, sick and in prison and you did not visit me." Then they also will answer, "Lord, when was it that we saw you hungry or thirsty or a stranger or naked or sick or in prison, and did not take care of you?" Then he will answer them, " Truly I tell you, just as you did not do it to one of the least of these, you did not do it to me."

Matthew 25:41-45

The only thing we can count on when we die is that our soul—our very being—will survive on this earth through the personal relationships we have experienced, the creations we have left behind, the communities in which we have lived, and the joy and sorrow to which we have given birth. That may very well be all there is, but that is a lot.

By assuming responsibility for our life's meaning, we also take control of our destiny. It may not be a pretty picture, or at least not the picture we had in mind when we began our pilgrimage. The search for meaning is not for the fainthearted. Now is the time to get on with our journey.

Happy Death

From Albert Camus we have learned that life is absurd, from Paul Tillich that we are separated, from Erich Fromm that having is vacuous, and from Jesus Christ that life without love and community is nothing. But even though no cosmic source of meaning has been revealed to us, we find ourselves drawn to the idea that the purpose of life is to die happy and that the only way to die happy is to learn how to be.

Individualism and the Search

*A*s a Christian, I certainly believe that God is more than just an option for my individual search. Rather God is actively impinging upon my life, in ways which I am often utterly unaware of and usually unsure of. Nevertheless, the search for meaning is not only what I do with myself. I am uncomfortable with "I am the captain of my ship; the master of my soul" language. Presumably, in writing our personal history, we discover that we are not only the sum of our actions, but we are also the result of other peoples' actions, maybe even God's actions. We do not arrive on the scene of the search for meaning without guides from the past, insights from others, and countless gifts along our way, including gifts from God.

THE PASTOR

In no sense are we equating dying happy with radical individualism or hedonism. This is not a superficial self-help, self-esteem, feel-good philosophy aimed at the "me" generation. To die happy we must first assume personal responsibility for the meaning of our life. Living means coming to terms with, rather than avoiding, spiritual, intellectual, emotional, and physical pain and suffering. To have a happy death we must confront meaninglessness and separation head on through being—resisting whenever possible the temptation merely to have. Being involves caring, loving, sharing, and participating in community with others.

In his account of Socrates' last day in prison, Plato suggests that the whole purpose of philosophy is to prepare us for death.

Those who really apply themselves in the right way to philosophy are directly and of their own accord preparing themselves for dying and death. If this is true, and they have actually been looking forward to death all their lives, it would of course be absurd to be troubled when the thing comes for which they have so long been preparing and looking forward.[4]

Philosophy, religion, and psychotherapy all help us prepare to die by teaching us how to be and how to care for our soul.

Polish mountain climber Wanda Rutkiewicz, the greatest woman high-altitude mountaineer of her time, may have experienced a happy death near the summit of Kangchenjunga along the border between Nepal and Sikkim in May 1992. Shortly before she died, Ms. Rutkiewicz was reported to have said, "For me to die up there will not be at all strange. It will be easy. After all, most of my friends are waiting for me there, in the mountains."[5] Somehow death on the icy slopes of Kangchenjunga seemed like a fitting climax to the life of a woman who had ascended eight of the world's fourteen highest peaks, including Everest, K2, and the Matterhorn. For Rutkiewicz life was about mountain-climbing. But she died among friends who, like herself, didn't make it back from that last great climb.

Twelve Ways to Die Unhappy

1. separated from yourself
2. separated from others
3. separated from the ground of your being
4. having never experienced real community
5. trying to have it all
6. keeping it all for yourself
7. marching to the beat of the wrong drummer
8. dancing to the wrong tune
9. fighting the wrong enemy
10. spending your life in a meaningless job
11. living your life as a series of accidents
12. denying your own mortality

Those who die happy scrupulously avoid being sucked into the seductive life-style of the living dead, who have traded their souls for a one-way ticket to oblivion. One reason so few of us die happy is that we refuse to plan for the one event in our life which is absolutely certain—our own death. Although few of us know either when we will die or how we will die, we do, nevertheless, have a number of options available to us as death approaches. For those of us who are into having, we can spend our final days reviewing our will, making certain that all of our worldly possessions will be distributed only to those who "deserve them most." Some of us may choose to pray for more time on earth, the salvation of our soul, and a risk-free eternity. Paraphrasing Irvin D. Yalom, we may choose to talk to others, give advice, say things we have been meaning to say before we die, take leave of others, be alone, weep, defy death, curse it, or be thankful for it.[6] Or we may savor the peace and contentment of knowing that we gave life our best shot and spend our remaining time with friends and loved ones putting the finishing touches on our soul.

Concerning God, death, and the search, Camus said, "There is but one freedom, to put oneself right with death. After that, everything is possible." We cannot force ourselves to believe in God. Belief in God involves coming to terms with death. When we have accepted death, "The problem of God will be solved—not the reverse."[7]

When all is said and done, according to Tillich,

The moment in which we reach the last depth of our lives is the moment in which we can experience the joy that has eternity within it, the hope that cannot be destroyed, and the truth on which life and death are built. For in the depth is truth; and in the depth is hope; and in the depth is joy.[8]

Whether our deserted island is a college campus, a large corporation, a failing marriage, a nursing home, or a homeless shelter, there is but one fundamental question: "How can I die happy?" Our answer will determine how we live and whether or not our life has meaning.

We wish you a meaningful journey through the rest of your life. But above all, "Die happy!"

Notes

Preface

1. Lewis H. Lapham, "Who and What Is American?" *Harper's Magazine* (January 1992), p. 46.

Introduction: THE LIVING DEAD

1. Parts of this chapter originally appeared in Thomas H. Naylor and Magdalena R. Naylor, "The Living Dead," *New Oxford Review* (September 1992), pp. 24-26. Copyright © 1992 *New Oxford Review*. Reprinted with permission from the *New Oxford Review* (1069 Kains Ave., Berkeley, CA 94706).
2. Albert Camus, *The Myth of Sisyphus and Other Essays* (New York: Alfred A. Knopf, 1955), p. 4.
3. Reinhold Niebuhr, *Christianity and Power Politics* (New York: Scribner's, 1940), p. 201.
4. J. Middleton Murry, cited in Reinhold Niebuhr, *Christianity and Power Politics* (New York: Scribner's, 1940), pp. 196-97.
5. Erich Fromm, *To Have or To Be* (New York: Harper & Row, 1976), p. XXVII.
6. Walker Percy, *Signposts in a Strange Land* (New York: Farrar, Straus and Giroux, 1991), p. 162.
7. Ibid., p. 163.
8. Elie Wiesel, *The Oath* (New York: Schocken, 1973), p. 11.

Chapter 1: A SEARCH PROCESS

1. Erich Fromm, *To Have or To Be* (New York: Harper & Row, 1976), p. 96.
2. Doron P. Levin, "Domino Founder Seizes Command," *New York Times* (December 10, 1991), p. D1.
3. Fromm, *To Have or To Be*, p. 97.
4. Cf. Viktor E. Frankl, *Man's Search for Meaning* (New York: Washington Square Press, 1984), p. 133.
5. Vaclav Havel, "The Power of the Powerless," in *The Power of the Powerless*, Vaclav Havel et al. (Armonk, N.Y.: M.E. Sharpe, 1990), p. 92.
6. Paul Tillich, *The Courage to Be* (New Haven: Yale University Press, 1952), p. 91.

Chapter 2: MEANINGLESSNESS

1. Jean-Paul Sartre, cited in R. Hepburn, "Questions About the Meaning of Life," *Religious Studies* 1 (1965), pp. 125-40.
2. Albert Camus, *The Rebel* (New York: Alfred A. Knopf, 1956), p. 5.
3. Irvin D. Yalom, *When Nietzsche Wept* (New York: Basic Books, 1992), p. 139.
4. Albert Camus, "Fourth Letter to a German Friend," July 1944, in Camus, *Resistance, Rebellion, and Death* (New York: Alfred A. Knopf, 1960), p. 28.
5. Albert Camus, *The Myth of Sisyphus and Other Essays* (New York: Alfred A. Knopf, 1955), p. v.
6. Albert Camus, *Caligula* (New York: Alfred A. Knopf, 1958), p. 8.
7. Albert Camus, "Return to Tipasa," in *The Myth of Sisyphus and Other Essays* (New York: Alfred A. Knopf, 1955), p. 203.
8. Albert Einstein, *Ideas and Opinions* (New York: Bonanza, 1954), p. 11.

Chapter 3: SEPARATION

1. Based on an article by Thomas H. Naylor entitled "Redefining Corporate Motivation, Swedish Style," *Christian Century* (May 30, 1990), pp. 566-69.
2. Paul Tillich, *The Shaking of the Foundations* (New York: Charles Scribner's Sons, 1948), pp. 156-57.
3. Rollo May, *Freedom and Destiny* (New York: Dell, 1981), pp. 10-11.
4. Ibid., p. 54.
5. Irvin D. Yalom, *When Nietzsche Wept* (New York: Basic Books, 1992), p. 177.
6. Erich Fromm, *Escape from Freedom* (New York: Avon, 1965), p. 161.
7. M. Scott Peck, *The Road Less Traveled* (New York: Touchstone, 1978), p. 44.
8. Reinhold Niebuhr, *Justice and Mercy*, ed. Ursula M. Niebuhr (New York: Harper & Row, 1976), p. v.
9. Tillich, *Shaking of the Foundations*, p. 57.
10. Erich Fromm, *The Art of Loving* (New York: Harper & Row, 1956), p. 88.
11. Jerold J. Keisman and Hal Straus, *I Hate You—Don't Leave Me* (New York: Avon, 1989), p. 4.
12. Sylvia Hewlett, *When the Bough Breaks* (New York: Basic Books, 1991), p. 14.
13. Yalom, *When Nietzsche Wept*, p. 55.
14. Ernest Becker, *The Denial of Death* (New York: Free Press, 1973).
15. John Ralstan Saul, *Voltaire's Bastards* (New York: Free Press, 1992), p. 347.

Chapter 4: HAVING

1. Lee Atwater, "Lee Atwater's Last Campaign," *Life* (February 1991).
2. Norman Lear, "Education for the Human Spirit," speech delivered to the National Education Association National Convention, Kansas City, Mo., July 7, 1990, p. 3.
3. Sylvia Nasar, "Even Among the Well-Off, the Richest Get Richer," *New York Times* (May 24, 1992).
4. Felicity Barringer, "Giving by the Rich Declines on Average," *New York Times* (May 24, 1992).
5. Graef S. Crystal, *In Search of Excess* (New York: W. W. Norton, 1991), pp. 27-28.
6. Lear, "Education," p. 7.
7. Alan Thein Durning, " Too Many Shoppers: What Malls and Materialism Are Doing to the Planet," *Washington Post* (August 24, 1992).

8. Michael McCloskey, *The Meaning of Life*, ed. David Friend (Boston: Little, Brown & Co., 1991), p. 13.
9. Stanley Hauerwas and William H. Willimon, *Resident Aliens: Life in the Christian Colony* (Nashville: Abingdon Press, 1989), pp. 77-78.
10. William H. Willimon, *Shaped by the Bible* (Nashville: Abingdon Press, 1990), pp. 28-29.
11. Hauerwas and Willimon, *Resident Aliens*, pp. 35-36.
12. Ramsey Clark, *The Nation* (July 15-22, 1992).
13. John Maynard Keynes, *Essays in Persuasion* (London: Macmillan, 1931), pp. 312-13.
14. Joan Robinson, *Economic Philosophy* (Chicago: Aldine, 1962), pp. 80-81.
15. John Maynard Keynes, *The General Theory of Employment, Interest, and Money* (London: Macmillan, 1936), p. 383.

Chapter 5: BEING

1. Ralph Waldo Emerson "Self-Reliance," in *Ralph Waldo Emerson: Selected Essays* (New York: Penguin, 1982), p. 177.
2. Reinhold Niebuhr, *Justice and Mercy*, ed. Ursula M. Niebuhr (New York: Harper & Row, 1976), p. v.
3. Rollo May, *The Courage to Create* (New York: Bantam, 1976), p. 15.
4. Ibid., p. 169.
5. Ibid., pp. 107-8.
6. Albert Camus, *The Rebel* (New York: Alfred A. Knopf, 1956), p. 253.
7. Vincent Van Gogh, quoted by Albert Camus in *The Rebel*, p. 257.
8. Robert Penn Warren, *Being Here* (New York: Random House, 1978), pp. 107-8.
9. M. Scott Peck, *The Road Less Traveled* (New York: Touchstone, 1978), p. 81.
10. Erich Fromm, *The Art of Loving* (New York: Harper & Row, 1989).
11. Irvin D. Yalom, *When Nietzsche Wept* (New York: Basic Books, 1992), p. 280.
12. Leah de Roulet, in *The Meaning of Life*, ed. David Friend (Boston: Little, Brown & Co., 1991), p. 16.
13. Raisa M. Gorbachev, *I Hope* (New York: HarperCollins, 1991), p. 97.
14. Ibid., p. 19.
15. Viktor Frankl, *Man's Search for Meaning* (New York: Washington Square Press, 1959), p. 135.
16. Janice Castro, " The Simple Life," *Time* (April 8, 1991), p. 58.
17. Frank Levering and Wanda Urbanska, *Simple Living* (New York: Viking, 1992).

Chapter 6: THE PERSONAL SEARCH

1. Vincent Barry, *Moral Issues in Business* (Belmont, Calif.: Wadsworth, 1979).
2. Laura L. Nash, "Ethics Without the Sermon," *Harvard Business Review* (November-December 1981), pp. 79-90.
3. Irvin D. Yalom, *When Nietzsche Wept* (New York: Basic Books, 1992), p. 188.

Chapter 7: THE LONGING FOR COMMUNITY

1. Albert Camus, *Notebooks 1942–1951* (New York: Alfred A. Knopf, 1965), p. 57.
2. Albert Einstein, *Out of My Later Years* (New York: Philosophical Library, 1950), p. 260.
3. Richard N. Goodwin, " The End of Reconstruction," *You Can't Eat Magnolias*, ed. H. Brandt Ayers and Thomas H. Naylor (New York: McGraw-Hill, 1972), p. 65.

4. Alan Thein Durning, "And Too Many Shoppers: What Malls and Materialism Are Doing to the Planet," *Washington Post* (August 24, 1992).
5. Lester Thurow, "Communitarian vs. Individualistic Capitalism," *The Responsive Community* (Fall 1992), pp. 24-25.
6. Some notion of the philosophy of St. Mark's can be gleaned from the book by James R. Adams, *So You Think You're Not Religious* (Cambridge, Mass.: Cowley, 1989).
7. Kirkpatrick Sale, *Human Scale* (New York: Coward, McCann & Geoghegan, 1989), pp. 487-90.
8. Theodore Roszak, *The Voice of the Earth* (New York: Simon & Schuster, 1992), p. 14.
9. Sale, *Human Scale*, p. 387.
10. Elizabeth O'Connor, *Servant Leaders, Servant Structures* (Washington, D.C.: Servant Leadership School, 1991).
11. Ibid., p. 68.
12. Ibid., p. 86.
13. Frank Bryan and John McClaughry, "From Vermont, a Radical Blueprint to Reinvigorate American Democracy," *Utne Reader* (January-February 1991), pp. 50-57.

Chapter 8: THE SEARCH FOR MEANING IN THE WORKPLACE

1. Albert Camus, *Notebooks 1935–1942* (New York: Paragon, 1991), p. 85.
2. Karl Marx, *Economic and Philosophical Manuscripts* (London: Lawrence and Wishart, 1959), p. 138.
3. Camus, *Notebooks*, p. 92.
4. Richard N. Goodwin, speech to the L. Q. C. Lamar Society in Memphis, Tenn., April 17, 1970. Quoted by Thomas H. Naylor, "A Southern Strategy," in *You Can't Eat Magnolias*, ed. H. Brandt Ayers and Thomas H. Naylor (New York: McGraw-Hill, 1972), p. 356.
5. IBM, *Business Conduct Guidelines* (Armonk, N.Y.: IBM, n.d., no copyright).
6. Kirkpatrick Sale, *Human Scale* (New York: Coward, McCann & Geoghegan, 1980), p. 352.
7. Andrew Pollack, "Japan Lures Auto Workers with 'Dream' Factories," *New York Times* (August 16, 1992), p. A1.
8. Jozef Tischner, *Etyka Solidarnosci* (Paris: Spotkania, 1982), pp. 18, 20.

Chapter 9: TOOLS FOR THE SEARCH

1. Lawrence Hartmann, "Presidential Address: Reflections on Human Values and Biopsychosocial Integration," *The American Journal of Psychiatry* (September 1992), p. 1136.
2. William Styron, *Darkness Visible* (New York: Vantage, 1992), p. 68.
3. Daniel Goleman, " Therapists See Religion as Aid, Not Illusion," *New York Times* (September 10, 1991).
4. Quoted in *Psychiatric News* (June 19, 1992), p. 20.
5. Irvin D. Yalom, *Existential Psychotherapy* (New York: Basic Books, 1980).
6. Jozef Tischner, *Etyka Solidarnosci* (Paris: Spotkania, 1982), p. 35.
7. Paul Tillich, *The Courage to Be* (New Haven, Conn.: Yale University Press, 1952), pp. 147-48.
8. Albert Camus, *Notebooks 1942–1951* (New York: Alfred A. Knopf, 1965), p. 39.
9. Albert Camus, *The Rebel* (New York: Alfred A. Knopf, 1956), pp. 255-56.
10. E. H. Erikson, *Young Man Luther: A Study in Psychoanalysis and History* (New York: W. W. Norton & Co., 1958), pp. 21-22.
11. Vaclav Havel, " The End of the Modern Era," lecture to the World Economic Forum, Davos, Switzerland, February 4, 1992.

12. Ibid.
13. Alfred North Whitehead, *Science and the Modern World* (New York: Macmillan, 1926), p. 267.

Chapter 10: SOUL CRAFTING

1. Adapted from William Ernest Henley's poem "Invictus."
2. Irvin D. Yalom, *When Nietzsche Wept* (New York: Basic Books, 1992), p. 140.
3. Albert Camus, *Notebooks 1942–1951* (New York: Alfred A. Knopf, 1965), p. 72.
4. Plato, " The Last Conversation: Phaedo," *The Last Days of Socrates* (New York: Penguin Books, 1969), p. 107.
5. Richard Cowper, "Woman Who Climbed too High," *Weekend Financial Times* (June 27-28, 1992).
6. Yalom, *When Nietzsche Wept*, p. 69.
7. Camus, *Notebooks 1942–1951*, p. 151.
8. Paul Tillich, " The Depth of Existence," in *The Shaking of the Foundations* (New York: Charles Scribner's Sons, 1948), p. 63.